of coexistence, which has always been marked by misperceptions and miscalculations. "The half dozen or so individuals in Washington and Moscow who decide how life-and-death power is used are like chess players in the dark," Barnet writes, "absorbed in a game they can barely see. Each player depends upon the other not to upset the table."

Now more Americans and Russians are talking to each other. Here is the dramatic story of the crucial new stage in their 60-year dialogue—how Nixon and Kissinger tried to transform the relationship and what kind of detente is likely to survive them.

Richard Barnet, co-author of *Global Reach* and author of five other books, including *The Roots of War* and *The Economy of Death*, was formerly with the Harvard Russian Research Center and was an adviser in the State Department during the Kennedy administration. He is a co-founder and co-director of the Institute for Policy Studies in Washington, D.C.

The Giants

Russia and America

RICHARD J. BARNET

SIMON AND SCHUSTER
NEW YORK

Designed by Irving Perkins
Manufactured in the United States of America
1   2   3   4   5   6   7   8   9   10

Library of Congress Cataloging in Publication Data

Barnet, Richard J.
    The giants.

    Bibliography: p.
    Includes index.
    1. United States—Foreign relations—Russia.
    2. Russia—Foreign relations—United States.
    3. Detente. I. Title.
JX1428.R8B36   327.73'047   77-9004

        ISBN 0-671-22741-6

For Julie, Beth and Mike

Contents

CHAPTER 1
Sixty Years of Coexistence

Robert Oppenheimer once compared the United States and the Soviet Union to two scorpions in a bottle, but the metaphor is not apt. True, each society has life-and-death power over the other, but the half dozen or so individuals in Washington or Moscow who decide how that power is to be used do not act by instinct. They are more like chess players in the dark, absorbed in a game they can barely see. Each player depends upon the other not to upset the table. Since neither quite knows what is happening on the board, each imputes to the other a master plan that tends to be a mirror image of his own. It is a dangerous game, but each uses it to define who he is.

The era of détente, or *razriadka* as the Russians call it—both words signify a relaxation or unwinding—is a new stage in the global contest Walter Lippmann dubbed the "cold war," in which the small group of politicians, diplomats, generals, and businessmen on each side are changing their relationships in complex and curious ways. At the heart of the controversy over détente is the question Tolstoy purported to settle in *War and Peace*: What difference do individuals make in great historical processes? Tolstoy thought that even the most powerful leaders were merely blind instruments in the grip of glacial historical forces. (If Napoleon had not existed, he would have been invented.) The skeptics of détente take much the same view, at least of the adversary, arguing that for all the clinking of glasses in the Kremlin, the Politburo retains its "master plan" to destroy the power of the United States and to succeed her as the number one nation. "Their objectives have not changed, only

9

their methods." Indeed, the skeptics say, their objectives cannot change. Soviet skeptics make precisely the same point about the unchanging nature of capitalists. The architects of détente, however, believe that a web of personal entanglements linking the elites who manage the two societies can lead to a moderation of the strategies of two competing empires in crucial ways. Helmut Sonnenfeldt, chief adviser on Soviet affairs during the Kissinger years, thinks that Americans have too long accepted the "Stalinist myth" of the "master plan." There's "nothing scientific" about their long-term strategy, despite their claims, he maintains. They adapt to circumstances, and the United States can have more influence by engaging them in a process of changing the circumstances. "The alternative," he says, "is a policy of isolation that will lead to war."

In the years of coexistence, especially since World War II, what each society has produced, how each has spent its money, how much freedom and dissent each has allowed, how much secrecy each has craved, and how each has treated the rest of the world have been substantially determined by what a roomful of men in the White House and the Kremlin thought their counterparts were doing or were about to do. The cold war has been a process of education of two rival elites, and détente is a new stage in that process.

For much of the last generation the managers of the global competition on both sides have believed that no fundamental improvement in U.S.-Soviet relations was possible without profound ideological conversion. Each projected that belief onto the other. "It must invariably be assumed in Moscow," George F. Kennan wrote in 1947, "that the aims of the capitalist world are antagonistic to the Soviet regime and, therefore, to the interests of the people it controls. If the Soviet government occasionally sets its signature to documents which would indicate the contrary, this is to be regarded as a tactical maneuver permissible in dealing with the enemy (who is without honor) and should be taken in the spirit of *caveat emptor*. Basically, the antagonism remains."

The official State Department view during most of the last generation was that personal relationships among U.S. and Soviet leaders—career diplomats liked to sneer at "summitry"—were more likely to be dangerous than productive. Henry Kissinger wrote in 1965 that "personal diplomacy" was a "futile" exercise, since whenever Soviet leaders "have had to make a choice between Western goodwill and territorial or political gain, they have unhesitatingly chosen the latter." Such a naïve and well-meaning American politician as Eisenhower might try to charm a tough Soviet boss like Khrushchev, but all that would result would be a short-lived agreement on "atmospherics." Soviet leaders were impressed by what they called "objective factors," not personalities. That is why the "Spirit of Geneva," the "Spirit of Camp David," and the "Spirit of Glassboro" seemed to evaporate within weeks, sometimes hours, of the communiqués that proclaimed them. The rhetoric of "peaceful coexistence" that the Russians promoted so vigorously was dangerous because it raised false hopes. When President Ford, under pressure from Ronald Reagan, tried to ban his predecessor's most successful slogan, it was a political reflex with much history behind it. John Foster Dulles used to warn against celebrating "relaxation of tension." After all, he would say, tension was not necessarily a bad thing. Democracies were easily lulled into letting down their guard. Henry Kissinger, in his *Nuclear Weapons and Foreign Policy,* published in 1957, warned that "peaceful coexistence" was merely "the most effective tactic" and "the best means to subvert the existing structure by means other than all-out war." In 1961 Professor Kissinger, in words his critics fifteen years later like to throw back at him, noted that "Communists advocate peace not for its own sake, but because the West is said to have grown so weak that it will go to perdition without a last convulsive upheaval." Richard Nixon summed up the abortive Kennedy détente of the summer of 1963—Khrushchev had given a warm response to the President's American University speech calling for a "relaxation of tensions"—by noting that "The bear is always most dangerous when he stands with arms open in friendship."

The Soviets periodically sound a contrapuntal theme. Ideological and cultural penetration from the West is a threat to their society. The danger of increased contact with the United States is that along with grain and high technology the Soviet Union will also import "inflation, decadence, and subversion." Soviet isolationism, the cult of the "closed society," to use the official U.S. designation of the Soviet system, was particularly strong in Stalin's day, but even now warnings are regularly to be found in theoretical journals and party speeches that détente carries certain vulnerabilities. Yet despite the suspicion on both sides that human contact can corrupt and confuse political judgment, more Americans and Russians are talking to one another than ever before. Indeed, the range and depth of contacts is perhaps the crucial distinguishing feature of the new stage in U.S.-Soviet relations that began in the Nixon administration.

Personal contacts help dissolve old stereotypes. Donald Kendall, president of Pepsico, an old Nixon friend, and a détente enthusiast, told a

Senate investigator how reassuring it was to discover that Soviet functionaries wear business suits, go to the opera, and confidentially, don't care much for the Cubans. "They're really just like us." Vladimir Alkhimov, Soviet deputy minister of trade, who with Kendall heads the American-Soviet Trade and Economic Council, told me the reason Americans and Russians make ideal trading partners is that "we are so much alike. We are both big countries and we like to do things on a big scale."

There is a naïve quality about such generalizations, yet direct communication, however superficial, seems preferable to the mutually reinforcing isolation within which American and Soviet leaders have tried to conduct their relationship during much of the past sixty years. It has been a political axiom in the United States since George Kennan pointed it out in his celebrated 1947 article in *Foreign Affairs* that Soviet leaders are prisoners of their own ideology, "which taught them that the outside world was hostile and that it was their duty eventually to overthrow the political forces beyond their borders." Stalin's world view, sustained, as Kennan put it, "by the powerful hands of Russian history and tradition," provided insulation from contrary ideological currents and reinforcement for whatever the Soviet ruler wanted to do to solidify his rule at home or to extend his power abroad. Capitalist encirclement, defined as the continuation on an international scale of the class struggle, which the triumph of Bolshevism had ended within the Soviet Union, was the justification for the continuation of dictatorial power and privilege of the Stalinist elite. Such a picture of an unalterably hostile world legitimized permanent sacrifice and permanent purge. It would not be lightly abandoned. But Soviet leaders could not forever cynically proclaim such a picture without having their own sense of reality corrupted. In the summer of 1946 Clark Clifford, who was then special counsel to President Truman, after consulting the Russian experts in the U.S. Government (including J. Edgar Hoover), summarized the official wisdom for the President in a secret report: the men in the Politburo were "isolated, largely ignorant of the outside world, blinded by adherence to Marxist dogma."

The ignorance, isolation, and ideological blindness of American leaders have understandably received much less attention in the United States, but they have been no less important factors in the relationship. George Kennan points out that from the start "American opinion-makers were poorly prepared" to understand what was going on in revolutionary Russia. The Bolshevik Revolution itself was "seriously misperceived" by reason of the widespread belief that the Bolshevik leaders were German agents.

A succession of Republican secretaries of state, taking the fiery rhetoric emanating from Moscow at face value, saw Lenin as an international conspirator instead of a revolutionary statesman. The Bolsheviks made no secret of their belief that the survival of the revolution in Russia and the achievement of peace and social justice in the world required the overthrow of capitalism everywhere, including the United States, and in the early years Soviet officials occasionally appealed to workers in capitalist countries to get rid of their oppressors. But Lenin was a realist who quickly perceived that this was not soon going to happen, and he, and Stalin more explicitly, concentrated efforts on building a revolutionary state in Russia that could survive in a capitalist world. In Washington, however, as has been frequently the case in U.S.-Soviet relations, words had more impact than deeds. Secretary of State Bainbridge Colby in 1920 said the United States would never recognize "the present rulers of Russia as a government with which the relations common to friendly governments can be maintained" because "the very existence of Bolshevism in Russia, the maintenance of their own rule, depends, and must continue to depend, upon the occurrence of revolutions in all other great civilized nations, including the United States."

Thus the United States and the Soviet Union began their sixty years of coexistence, each persuaded that the other was out to destroy its social system. For their part, the Bolsheviks were convinced that the dispatch of three American battalions to Archangel to serve with a British and French interventionary force during the civil war was in pursuit of Churchill's plot "to strangle Bolshevism in its cradle." George Kennan, in his two-volume study of the period, ascribes more limited purposes to the intervention, just as most historians ascribe to Lenin operational goals far more modest than world revolution. But it was the image, not the reality, that sustained fear on both sides. The conservative politicians in charge of defining the American national interest shared one idea with their Bolshevik counterparts: the world was not big enough for both to maintain their power. The very existence of two such radically antithetical social systems threatened the survival of each.

By the early 1920s, however, the reality if not the rhetoric of coexistence was accepted on both sides. This did not mean that the State Department accepted the legitimacy of the Soviet regime, even after diplomatic relations with Russia were restored in 1933—indeed, Nixon, it could be argued, was the first President to acknowledge that an unreformed and unrepentant Soviet Union could be a responsible actor on the world stage

—but it did mean that Soviet power over a sixth of the earth's surface was a recognized fact of international life. So, too, the Bolsheviks quickly reassessed the strength of world capitalism and concluded that its most advanced embodiment, the United States, would be around a long time.

For sixty years two national elites have been trying to define the ground rules of coexistence. Because the corporation lawyers, bankers, small-town politicians, and occasional professor who decided what the American national interest was started with such a different set of premises and experiences from the revolutionaries and Communist party *apparatchiki* who defined Soviet interests, some monumental misunderstandings about one another were bound to occur. In the United States the official view was that the Soviets were inscrutable, a riddle wrapped in a mystery inside an enigma, as Churchill said. In the Soviet Union conventional wisdom was precisely the opposite. The United States was an open book, an imperialist power whose moves could be explained by recourse to "scientific social- ism." In fact, the Soviets were never quite the mystery to the American national security establishment its leaders liked to claim. (The "closed society" rhetoric was helpful in establishing the legitimacy of overflights and sophisticated espionage efforts behind the Iron Curtain.) Nor were the Soviets really as confident as they pretended to be that they understood America. (Soviet analysts, as more than one researcher at the Academy of Sciences Institute for the Study of the U.S.A. and Canada admitted to me, had great difficulty in fitting the enormous profusion of complex informa- tion into the proper ideological boxes.)

The cold war has fed on misunderstanding, but it is not the product of misunderstanding. In retrospect it seems inevitable that America and Russia should have clashed at the midpoint of the twentieth century. Alexis de Tocqueville ended *Democracy in America* (1835) with a prediction that the center of world power would shift from a declining Europe to the two great non-European continental superpowers. In *The Expansion of England,* written at the height of the Victorian empire (1883), Sir John Seeley predicted that America and Russia, already "enormous political aggregations," would "completely dwarf such European states as France and Germany and depress them into a second class." Geoffrey Barraclough argues, in *An Introduction to Contemporary History,* that the two Europe- centered world wars of this century merely delayed a historical process long under way whereby world power would be delivered into the hands of the two *arriviste* empires. (Hitler, he notes, warned in 1928 that if Germany did not want to end up as "a second Holland or a second

Switzerland" it must move quickly, because "with the American Union a new power of such dimensions has come into being as threatens to upset the whole former power and order of rank of the states.") However far back one cares to trace it, by the end of the Second World War the shift of power that De Tocqueville and many others had predicted was complete.

A buoyant America fresh from a successful global military campaign, her economy restored by the very catastrophe that doomed the European empires, enemies and allies alike, faced a grievously wounded Soviet Union that had expanded its power into the heart of Europe. Looking back thirty years, it is hard to believe that the two legatees of Europe's power could have avoided their monumental rivalry even if Lenin had never left Geneva. That at least is now the private view of younger Soviet scholars, who seem to have no patience for debating who started the cold war. A junior researcher at the Academy of Sciences told me that a well-known American revisionist account of the early cold-war years had been published in the Soviet Union about ten years ago, "but we would never publish it now." In the era of détente it is better to look at Soviet-American relations "objectively" and avoid laying blame. (Official Soviet historiography, however, continues to defend every twist and turn of Soviet foreign policy over the last forty years.)

Nonetheless, if the managers of the two expanding empires were fated to be rivals, for reasons of geopolitics as well as ideology, the crises of the past generation have been magnified by misperceptions. Both elites have been poorly prepared for the rigors of coexistence. Miscalculations on the other side are easier for us to see. Soviet moves in Korea in 1950 and in Cuba in 1962 were made on the assumption that the U.S. leaders would respond quite differently from the way they actually did. Whether Stalin ordered North Korean troops to invade South Korea, or, as Khrushchev recalls in his memoirs, acquiesced in the plan of Kim Il Sung, the North Korean leader, for a quick catalytic incursion to spark a revolution (much like the CIA's plan for the Bay of Pigs), he could not have counted on what happened. Not only did the United States make an unanticipated commitment of ground troops to an area Secretary of State Dean Acheson had declared six months earlier to be outside the U.S. "defense perimeter," thus raising the specter of a U.S.-Soviet war—Soviet sources now admit that Russians were flying MIGs in combat with American pilots—but, more important, the Korean crisis created the psychological and political climate for bringing about the one thing Stalin feared most—German rearmament. (Recently a Soviet general who is a member of the SALT delegation after a few vodkas with his U.S. counterpart gave the confused signals on Korea in 1950 as an example of the "dangerous unpredicta-bility" of U.S. policy. It was unfair to be "misleading," he said.) Twelve years after the Korean invasion Nikita Khrushchev, despite a personal meeting with Kennedy, or perhaps because of it, profoundly miscalculated the young President's reaction to the Cuban missile ploy. The result was a humiliation for the Soviet Union and the collapse of Khrushchev's personal power.

But the American misperceptions and miscalculations are no less ironical. Dean Acheson talked about building "situations of strength" to im-prove the diplomatic position of the West at a time when the Soviet Union was still bleeding from the war, and the United States, with a monopoly on nuclear weapons, would never again be so far ahead of the Soviet Union in military and economic power. "The period of American monopoly of the bomb," Professor Adam Ulam of Harvard writes in his *Expansion and Coexistence,* "was the period of the greatest Soviet pushfulness in foreign policy, of the rapid satellitization of Eastern Europe and of the Communist conquest of China." The American elite, George Kennan now argues, mis-understood Stalin's attitude toward nuclear weapons.

> There is no reason to doubt that Stalin saw this weapon as he himself described it: as something with which one frightened people with weak nerves. . . . Indeed, in view of the physical dangers the weapon presented, and the confusion which its existence threw over certain cherished Marxist concepts as to the way the world was supposed to work, he probably would have been quite happy to see it removed entirely from national arsenals, including his own, if this could be done without the acceptance of awkward forms of international in-spection. . . . Little of this was perceived, however, on the Western side—and on the American side in particular.

If George Kennan is right, the American misunderstanding about the effect of nuclear weapons on Soviet thinking is perhaps the most fateful miscalculation of history. It is the most dramatic example of how difficult it has been in the nuclear age for great empires to grow political power in gun barrels. Until 1968 or so the United States had a consistently larger, more modern, and presumably more effective nuclear force than the Soviet Union. (It is still "ahead," although the Soviet stockpiles are so large the term has lost its meaning.) But the superiority could not be harnessed to political goals. It was merely a spur to the Soviets to catch up. During these years the United States underestimated its sources of real political strength. Despite the awesome nuclear arsenal at their command, both Dean Acheson and John Foster Dulles failed to exploit their biggest "bargaining chip" of all (to use the current Kissinger term), Soviet fear of German rearmament. The reason, as Professor Ulam puts it in his history of the period, was timidity. "Next to an all-out war, the prospect of negotiating with the Communists inspired the most fear in the bosom of American diplomats." On March 10, 1952, Stalin offered to accept a unified, rearmed but neutral Germany, a move clearly designed to stop NATO and West German rearmament but one which made some important concessions to the United States. But the State Department, now thoroughly committed to the integration of West Germany into NATO, dismissed the offer as a trick. Whether Stalin was "sincere"—he was usually sincere when it came to defining his own interests, and he had reason to pay a high price to avoid a hostile German army on his border—or whether the recession of Soviet power from East Germany would have been worth the price, we shall never know. This crucial episode in postwar diplomacy is worth remembering as an example of how American national security managers preferred to live with their own image of the adversary rather than discover the reality through the painful process of personal engagement.

That process, says Helmut Sonnenfeldt, who calculates that he has spent almost two hundred hours with Brezhnev, is perhaps the most important aspect of the new relationship. "We understand them better because of our contact with the top leaders. They are a little less mysterious, less forbidding." The result, he says, is that American negotiators are more confident than in Dulles' day.

CHAPTER 2
Détente: How It Happened

At 11:00 P.M. on October 24, 1973, Henry Kissinger convened an emergency meeting at the White House to study what the Soviet ambassador had called a "very urgent" communication from Chairman Brezhnev. Thirty minutes later the first worldwide military alert since 1962 had begun. The aircraft carrier *John F. Kennedy* headed at full speed for the Mediterranean. The 82nd Airborne Division, based at Fort Bragg, North Carolina, was ordered to be ready within five hours for immediate duty in the Middle East. The Strategic Air Command in charge of the B-52s and strategic missiles aimed at the Soviet Union was placed on an advanced state of alert. (There are five degrees of military alert, ranging from DefCon [Defense Condition] 5, the normal peacetime state, to DefCon 1, which is war. That night most units were placed on DefCon 3, but the Sixth Fleet, patrolling the Mediterranean, was put on DefCon 2.) Kissinger informed Lord Cromer, the British ambassador, of the show of force in the making, and he is said to have replied testily, "Why tell us, Henry? Tell your friends the Russians." By 7:30 the next morning the CIA had sent the White House a report that a Soviet ship suspected of carrying nuclear weapons had just docked at Port Said. A few hours later Kissinger was asked at a press conference whether the alert "might have been prompted as much by American domestic requirements as by the requirements of diplomacy in the Middle East." (Nixon's "Saturday night massacre" of the Watergate special prosecutor and those who felt squeamish about firing him had occurred a few days before.) In a tone of sorrow the secretary of state dismissed as a "symptom of what is happening to our country" the suggestion that Watergate rather than the Russians was behind the crisis. Noting that "we possess, each of us, nuclear arsenals capable of annihilating humanity," he warned the Russians not to "transplant the great power rivalry into the Middle East." The Russians, he said, should fulfill their "special duty to see to it that confrontations are kept within bounds that do not threaten civilized life." Twenty-four hours later, after a flurry of messages between Washington and Moscow, the alert was over and the crisis had passed.

What had happened to reproduce the familiar drama of the cold war— the nighttime congregation of black limousines at the White House West Gate, tight-lipped officials waving aside the press, more officials poring over telegrams in search of a "signal" from Moscow that could mean peace or war—at the height of what everyone then called détente? Richard Nixon, the man who had proclaimed that the era of confrontation had given way to the era of negotiation, described the events as "the most difficult crisis we had since the Cuban missile crisis of 1962."

Two weeks after the outbreak of the Yom Kippur War, which began on October 6, 1973, the Israelis had turned the tide and threatened to trap 100,000 Egyptian soldiers in the Sinai Peninsula. The United States and the Soviet Union had been cooperating in seeking a cease-fire. On October 24 Brezhnev sent a message to Nixon on the hot line, proposing: "If the Israelis are not going to adhere to the cease-fire, let us work together to impose a cease-fire, if necessary by force." At the same time coded messages between Cairo and Damascus were intercepted in Washington. Anwar Sadat cabled President Assad of Syria: "I understand your position, and accept that you may think it necessary to request Soviet troops if you think the situation calls for it." According to Mohammed Heikel's inside account (Heikel was editor of *Al Ahram* and had been one of Nasser's closest confidants), the Syrian president did request Soviet troops on October 24, although he denied it in a telegram to Sadat. The Egyptian president cabled back: "We ourselves have never requested Soviet forces but only Soviet observers to take part in supervision of the cease-fire. The Soviet Union has already sent seventy observers. I have so informed Waldheim."

The intercepted messages with their ambiguous requests for Soviet troops reinforced by a direct Soviet proposal to the United States for joint military action to impose the peace, and the appearance of Soviet transport planes flying toward Cairo, were interpreted by Kissinger as a threat of "unilateral action" requiring a dramatic response. "We obtained information," Nixon said later, "which led us to believe that the Soviet Union was planning to send a very substantial force into the Middle East—a military force." At a press conference on the day of the crisis Secretary of Defense James Schlesinger admitted that there were "mixed reactions and different assessments" of the likelihood that the Soviets would make a unilateral move. In any event, once faced with the alert, the Soviets changed their position and called for the exclusion of the superpowers from the Middle East peace force.

The fifteen-hour crisis offers a view of the global relationship of the United States and the Soviet Union in microcosm. All the principal elements that make the relationship possible and those that threaten it were present. In October 1973 the United States and the Soviet Union were antagonists as well as collaborators. Each was ready to sacrifice the interests of its Middle East clients to the mutual overriding interests of both in avoiding war. As always, evidence of intentions was hard to read, and in Washington evidence of Soviet intentions was misread. There was little likelihood that the Soviets would land an expeditionary force in the Middle East over American objections, and Kissinger's fear, which he later expressed, that the Soviets were about to dominate the Middle East and "use it as a base to communize West Europe and Japan" had no basis in reality. (A few months later the Soviets had suffered a dramatic loss of influence in the region.) Barely four months after the second Nixon-Brezhnev summit meeting, at which the two leaders reaffirmed their pledges of peaceful coexistence and cooperation, the U.S. secretary of defense publicly welcomed the chance to prove "the ability of the United States to react appropriately, firmly, and quickly."

In the background were considerations of domestic American politics, the fear that the disarray of Watergate would weaken America's capacity to project its power and thereby embolden the adversary. Also evident was the inherent conflict between managing a tightly controlled adversary relationship with the Soviet Union and giving due deference to the West European allies (who didn't believe in the crisis and were annoyed at not being consulted). Overselling détente had led to the overselling of the crisis. But overshadowing all these considerations was the durability of the new U.S.-Soviet relationship. With the sudden passing of the crisis the mutual effort in Washington and Moscow to improve relations, to expand economic, cultural, and scientific cooperation, and to control arms was resumed.

Richard Nixon himself was struck by the irony that he, the first American politician to reach the White House as an apostle of anticommunism, should be the President to make peace with Russia. He reminded his hosts in the Kremlin at the 1972 Moscow summit, where the twelve basic principles of détente and the first SALT agreement on arms limitation were signed, "I have the reputation of being a hard line anti-communist." In memos for the President written after the 1972 visits to Moscow and Peking, Bob Haldeman wrote, "Only Nixon could have done it." Clark Clifford, who advised Truman on how to win the election of 1948 and ever since has been thinking about how passions are translated into votes, agrees. "Richard Nixon was the first American President since the war who didn't have to worry about Richard Nixon."

The Richard Nixon that Richard Nixon did not have to worry about was a consummate master of the politics of anticommunism. The early red-baiting campaigns against Jerry Voorhis, an early consumer advocate, and Helen Gahagan Douglas, an energetic New Dealer, succeeded in making each look to California voters as better suited to membership in the Supreme Soviet than in the U.S. Congress. The "lonely fight" against Alger Hiss was a morality play. The young congressman took on a generation—Hiss became the symbol of F.D.R. and the New Deal—and triumphed by producing the "pumpkin papers," microfilms of largely innocuous documents buried on Whittaker Chambers' Maryland farm. Senator Nixon's best known legislative accomplishment was the Mundt-Nixon Act, a piece of repressive legislation to keep the country pure of suspected subversives. Nixon perfected the rhetoric of right-wing anti-communism. In the 1952 campaign, when he was running for Vice-President with Dwight D. Eisenhower, he lashed out at "Dean Acheson's College of Cowardly Communist Containment," repeating the charge that the Truman administration had sold out to communism by being insufficiently tough. In his second term as Vice-President, at a time when Premier Khrushchev was about to visit the United States, Nixon characterized the Soviet system as one with the object of "not only continued domination over its own people but eventual world domination—by war if necessary, by other means, if possible."

At the same time, Nixon was much too shrewd to identify himself fully with the extremists in his own party. He knew how to display that peculiar blend of *gravitas* and flexibility that distinguishes those who are to be trusted with power from those, such as Barry Goldwater, who are admired for the sincerity of their convictions. As Eisenhower's Vice-President at the time of the first post-Stalin thaw, the "Spirit of Geneva" that emerged briefly from the first summit conference since Potsdam, Nixon made statesmanlike appeals: "The time has arrived for all of us to settle our differences peacefully at the conference table so that we will not run the risk of eventually settling them on the battlefield in a war no one wants." Although in a 1955 speech he called for the use of nuclear weapons in case of a new war in Indochina and had refurbished his image as an anticommunist crusader by holding an impromptu "kitchen debate" with Khrushchev in 1959 and being stoned by leftist mobs in Caracas, he ran for President as a moderate against John F. Kennedy. In a televised debate he chided Kennedy for even thinking of such a thing as invading Cuba to get rid of Castro, because such a course implied violations of international law. (He was at the time the White House action officer for the planning of the Bay of Pigs operation.)

By the time he was ready to run for the presidency again he had rearranged his foreign policy views into a more or less coherent pattern. A year before the 1968 election he published an article in *Foreign Affairs* entitled "Asia after Vietnam" in which he identified the United States as a "Pacific power" and telegraphed two ideas that were to become cornerstones of his foreign policy. One was the notion that "we simply cannot afford to leave China forever outside the family of nations, there to nurture its fantasies, cherish its hates, and threaten its neighbors. There is no place on this small planet for a billion of its potentially most able people to live in angry isolation." The other idea was "that the role of the United States as a policeman is likely to be limited in the future." In embryonic form he spelled out what was to become the "Nixon Doctrine": the use of local forces against communist revolutions (vietnamization), avoidance of direct confrontations between the nuclear powers, and the buildup of regional powers as deputy peace-keepers.

In his *Foreign Affairs* article Nixon made it clear that for all his years of service in the Europe-oriented Eisenhower administration, he identified himself with the Asian wing of the Republican party. The greatest danger to America in the final third of the twentieth century was "Asia, not Europe or Latin America." When he spoke of his "long-range aim" to "pull China back into the family of nations" he said nothing about playing China off against the Soviet Union, which was the essence of his later policy. Henry Kissinger liked to treat the 1967 article as a seminal document, saying that it "really foreshadowed the Peking initiative"—but that seems overly generous. Nixon had said that "the world cannot be safe until China changes." By the time the presidential party arrived at the Great

Wall five years later, American perceptions of China had changed a good deal but Chinese foreign policy had not.

Henry Kissinger was thoroughly identified with the European wing of the Republican party, which had helped to forge the bipartisan foreign policy in the Truman administration and had loyally supported it all through the McCarthy era. Protégé of Nelson Rockefeller, the symbol of the Europe-oriented Eastern Establishment, his career launched by a book published under the auspices of the Council on Foreign Relations, a student of modern European history, Kissinger, except for two brief trips to South Vietnam in 1965 and 1966 for Ambassador Henry Cabot Lodge, had had virtually no experience outside Europe. His academic preoccupations had been NATO and nuclear weapons. He shared the conventional wisdom about the Soviet threat and what the United States should do about it. Indeed, in *Nuclear Weapons and Foreign Policy* he helped to articulate the new bipartisan consensus. The Soviet Union and China, he wrote then, were "revolutionary powers," not because of their internal social system but because they "do not accept the framework of the international order or the domestic structure of other states or both." Peaceful coexistence, he warned, was "an offensive tactic . . . the best means to subvert the existing structure by means other than all-out war." A "status quo power," such as the United States, he noted, is tempted "to gear its policy to the expectation of a fundamental change of heart of its opponent" and to expect "a basic change in Communist society and aims." The Soviets have pursued détente at least five different times since 1917, Kissinger wrote in 1965, and each time the period of relaxation came to an end "when an opportunity for expanding communism presented itself." In *Nuclear Weapons and Foreign Policy* and in *The Troubled Partnership* Kissinger warned that unless negotiations with the Soviet Union were subordinated to the primary interest of the "North Atlantic community," rivalries within Europe and between America and Europe would "either paralyze negotiations or enable the Soviet Union to use them to demoralize the West." Eleven years later Jimmy Carter campaigned for President on the charge that "the lone ranger" with the German accent had abandoned America's traditional allies in Europe in the pursuit of an elusive détente.

How did it happen that a man who had made his reputation as a theorist of the art of confronting Soviet power and ideology should become the architect of a new negotiated relationship with the Kremlin rooted in the entanglements of peace? By January 1969, when he took over the basement room directly under the Oval Office and began to mesh his evolving world view with Nixon's political instincts, Kissinger had come to look upon the Soviet Union as a "legitimate" rather than a "revolutionary" power. Partly his change of perception had to do with the Sino-Soviet dispute; it was based on a growing realization that the clash of Soviet and Chinese state interests had broken the ideological bonds of "world communism." Partly Kissinger's changed evaluation of the Soviet Union dated from the Cuban missile crisis of 1962, when the Soviet leaders, in the cliché inevitably used to describe the event, "looked into the abyss." (John F. Kennedy had looked too, and though he knew the United States had overwhelming superiority in nuclear weapons, he had estimated the probability that hundreds of millions of people, including a good many Americans, might be killed as "between one out of three and even.") In the post-crisis atmosphere Khrushchev agreed to a partial test-ban treaty and seemed eager to reduce the tension that defined U.S.-Soviet relations. President Kennedy, without letting the old Russian hands at the State Department see it, drafted an extraordinary speech, which he gave on June 10, 1963, at American University in Washington. Soviet citizens found it electrifying. For months some carried clippings of it in their wallets. It was an appeal for an end to the cold war, the first speech by an American President in more than a decade and a half to mention that the people of the Soviet Union were human beings and to pay tribute to their bravery and suffering in the war. It marked the first official attempt to exorcise the devil theory that determined official attitudes and public opinion toward the Soviet Union. In the secrecy with which it was prepared, in the themes it struck, the J.F.K. speech was a harbinger of the Nixon-Kissinger détente.

By the time the Nixon administration took office the mini-détente that began in the last months of Kennedy's life had already suffered severe strains, principally because of the escalation of the Vietnam War and the U.S. invasion of the Dominican Republic in 1965 and the Soviet invasion of Czechoslovakia in 1968. But Kissinger had come to the conclusion that U.S. policy toward Russia should be geared to long-term interests rather than the "atmospherics" generated by particular crises or their resolutions. There were changes in what the Russians like to call "objective conditions" which required a new policy toward the Soviet Union. Indeed, the analysis Kissinger and his staff made in 1969 about the changes in the "correlation of forces" in the world is remarkably similar to the analysis that the Soviets themselves were making at the time.

Barely four years earlier, imperial rhetoric was at flood tide. "We are the number one nation," Lyndon Johnson proclaimed, and "we intend to stay number one." Six hundred thousand troops in Vietnam, more massive aerial bombardments than had taken place in all of World War II, the Dominican invasion—the United States, "guardian at the gates of world freedom," was lashing out around the world, fighting what Walt Rostow, who was Johnson's Kissinger, said might well be the war to end all war. But the postwar foreign policy consensus had broken under the strain. Johnson was driven from office. The Vietnamese demonstrated that they understood American politics better than American politicians. ("The more American soldiers who come," a Vietnamese diplomat told me in 1967, "the sooner they will all leave." It sounded like a prayer, but it was a prediction.) The complacent advice offered by the Pentagon and the old Russian hands such as Llewellyn Thompson at the time of the Cuban missile crisis had proved wrong too. The conventional wisdom had it that Khrushchev would survive the humiliation and the Soviets would not challenge the United States in missiles. But by 1968 Khrushchev's successors were well on the way to matching the number of U.S. land-based missiles and had built up a fleet of submarines equipped with nuclear rockets. In its effort to prove its "will" and "determination" in Vietnam the United States was giving a daily demonstration of the limitations of its military power and the problems of a democratic system in fighting unpopular foreign wars.

In an article published shortly before he took office Kissinger laid out the new realities that confronted the planners of U.S. foreign policy:

> The United States is no longer in a position to operate programs globally . . . our contributions should not be the sole or principal effort, but it should make the difference between success and failure . . . Regional groupings supported by the United States will have to take over major responsibility for their immediate areas, with the United States being concerned more with the overall framework of order than with the management of every regional enterprise.

A direct confrontation with the Soviet Union was to be avoided. The United States no longer had either the power or the will to police what Kissinger had once called the "gray areas" of the world.

The second change in the "correlation of forces" was the Sino-Soviet dispute. In 1961 Kissinger was still talking about a "Sino-Soviet bloc" despite the fact that the dispute was no longer concealed. In 1959 Khrushchev had asked President Eisenhower at their meeting at Camp David if he would like to talk about Red China, implying, as Eisenhower says in his memoirs, "that he had been specifically asked to bring up the subject with me." But Eisenhower replied that there was little use in talking about such an unpleasant matter "for the simple reason that Red China had put herself beyond the pale so far as the United States was concerned." By 1969 Kissinger was aware—because the Chinese had announced it in 1963 —that Khrushchev just before visiting Eisenhower had abrogated a nuclear sharing agreement with Peking (as a "presentation gift" to the American President, the Chinese charged) and that the Chairman was trying to reach an agreement with the United States to keep nuclear weapons out of the hands of both China and Germany. The Johnson administration, especially Secretary of State Dean Rusk, was implacably hostile to the Chinese. Rusk, unable to understand the Vietnamese revolution, was convinced that China was the source of the aggression in Indochina. Defense Secretary Robert McNamara called "Long Live the Victory of People's War" by General Lin Piao China's *Mein Kampf*. President Kennedy, according to Joseph Alsop (who occasionally was privy to inside information of this sort), "had ordered exploration of the idea of destroying . . . the Chinese nuclear program," and the idea continued to intrigue Pentagon officials until mid-1966, when the Chinese detonated their third bomb, a 200-kiloton thermonuclear device. Kissinger believed that the differences between the Soviets and the Chinese could be exploited. (As early as 1955 he had talked of "our primary task of dividing the U.S.S.R. and China.") Barely six months after moving to Washington he gave a background briefing at San Clemente in which he explained the connection between the Sino-Soviet rivalry and a U.S.-Soviet détente.

> The deepest international conflict in the world today is not between U.S. and the Soviet Union, but between the Soviet Union and Communist China. Therefore, one of the positive prospects in the current situation is that whatever the basic intentions of Soviet leaders, confronted with the prospect of a China growing in strength and not lessening in hostility, they may want a period of détente in the West . . . because they do not wish to be in a position in which they have to confront major crises on both sides of their huge country over an indefinite period of time.

The third factor that helped to change Kissinger's view of how to handle the Russians was the collapse of the American foreign policy consensus. That consensus, which had been a source of enormous strength for the

managers of U.S. foreign policy, had rested on a self-image of altruism—
"We have no quarrel with the Communists," Secretary of State Dean Rusk
once put it; "all our quarrels are on behalf of other people." But the
nightly ritual of watching napalmed children, cowering refugees, and
burned huts on television—all advertised as part of an American rescue
mission—had shattered that image for a significant number of Americans.
"The American mood," Kissinger warned in his last article before assum-
ing office, "oscillates dangerously between being ashamed of power and
expecting too much of it." The self-confidence that made crusading anticommunism a politically viable policy for the United States in the first
postwar generation was gone and with it the credibility for fighting the
cold war in old ways. The old consensus depended upon a disarmingly
simple view of the world. There were two camps, to use Stalin's term, the
Free World (and a few nervous neutrals) on one side and the communist
monolith on the other. But now the Soviet Union itself had to contend
with restless communist countries of Eastern Europe—such independent
and wary ones as Yugoslavia and overtly hostile ones like Albania and
China.

There was a fourth reason to believe that the "correlation of forces"
in the world was shifting, although in 1969 Kissinger, who liked to advertise his distaste for economics, was only dimly aware of it. By the end of
the 1960s American economic preeminence was coming to an end.
Though it was and is still the world's strongest economic power, the gap
between the U.S. economy and the recovered economies of Western
Europe and Japan had closed. This reality, which in a general sense was
expected and even planned for at the end of World War II when the
United States undertook its major aid programs, was reflected in sharpened
trade competition and in the weakening of the dollar in international
money markets. The $100 billion war in Indochina, superimposed upon
an already massive military budget, was producing some serious strains in
the U.S. economy and with it a growing awareness that there were limits
on the resources America could devote to fighting the cold war on a
global scale.

In several respects Henry Kissinger changed his ideas about managing
U.S.-Soviet relations from the hard-line views on which he had made his
academic reputation. One basic view persisted, however. Throughout his
eight years in power Kissinger would periodically seek to remind the
Soviet leaders in pointed ways of America's military might. The worldwide alert was one example; the bombing and mining of Haiphong just

before the Moscow summit was another. "The Russians," he said in a background briefing in defense of the Cambodian "incursion" of May–June 1970, "will judge us by the general purposefulness of our performance everywhere." But while military power still played a dominant role in the U.S.-Soviet relationship, he insisted, it had to be used more selectively and in counterpoint to nonmilitary approaches.

Having spent most of his academic career deploring the lack of a conceptual framework for American foreign policy and urging that "we put our intellectual house in order," Kissinger came to the White House with some conceptual notions on which to base a policy and a few ideas for experimentation. One idea that immediately intrigued Nixon and Kissinger —they discussed it at their first meeting at the Hotel Pierre when the President-elect interviewed the professor for a possible position in the new administration—was that the Russians should be persuaded to put pressure on the North Vietnamese to make peace. It was a naïve idea, not because the Russians wouldn't try it—in February 1965 Kosygin went to Hanoi to urge negotiations with the United States at the moment the American Air Force began bombing the North Vietnamese capital, and the Kremlin pressed for concessions once again in Johnson's December 1965 "peace offensive" and bombing lull—but because the Vietnamese, who had their own revolutionary theory, their own timetable, and their own thousand-year history of maintaining independence from enemies and protectors alike, could not be moved. Nevertheless, even to make the experiment required a revision of the official view of the Soviet Union. No longer a "revolutionary" power bent on upsetting the chessboard, the U.S.S.R. was now playing the traditional diplomatic game. The hunch that by 1969 the Soviet Union wanted to see the Vietnam War ended on whatever terms possible was right. I remember meeting Georgi Arbatov, the head of the Institute for the Study of the U.S.A. and the leading academic theorist of détente in the Soviet Union, a few days after Nixon's election and being taken aback by his view of the Vietnam War. Not a word about the "great revolutionary struggle" or the "indomitable will of the Vietnamese people"; just "Let us get rid of this unpleasant incident. It is not important enough to disturb relations between two great nations."

So the first conceptual revision was to treat the Soviet Union as a "status quo" power and hope that they would play the assigned part. By and large, it turned out to be an accurate characterization of the role to which the men in the Kremlin aspired and which, given a chance, they were prepared to play. The new view of the Soviet Union required a revision of official eschatology. The Acheson-Dulles view was that the Soviet Union was a relentlessly expansionist power that would push out from its huge periphery wherever countervailing force was not present. No negotiations were possible except in the most secondary matters, because each concession offered by the West became the starting point for the next Soviet demand. These were the famous "salami tactics" about which a whole generation of diplomats warned. The ultimate Soviet aim was to take over the world—to communize it, some said, to achieve global geopolitical domination, others argued—and that being so, it hardly made sense to be friendly. When the Soviets made efforts to correct these impressions—by making disarmament proposals, orchestrating peace offensives, or even by making occasional substantial concessions—the prevailing State Department view was that the Kremlin was now more dangerous than ever because it was out to lull public opinion and to divide the West. Official hope of avoiding war lay in a change of heart inside the Kremlin. The optimistic assumption, never stated, was that somehow time was on America's side.

In one of his last articles before going to Washington, Kissinger took on the question of Soviet intentions, whether they had changed, whether they could change. "The obsession with Soviet intentions," he wrote, "causes the West to be smug during periods of tension and usually evokes purely military counter-measures." Both American hawks and doves, he wrote, "are at one that a settlement presupposes a change in the Soviet system." The hawks say it will inevitably come, and the doves say it has already taken place. But, Kissinger argued, "if we focus our policy discussions on Soviet purposes, we confuse the debate . . . Soviet trends are too ambiguous to offer a reliable guide—it is possible that not even Soviet leaders fully understand the dynamics of their system." Once in office he made the decision to base American policy on an assessment of short-term concrete interests, American and Soviet, rather than on ultimate goals. It was doubtless the most important conceptual innovation he made in developing U.S. foreign policy toward the Soviet Union. "Henry is as anti-Soviet as they come. He hates the bastards!" a high White House official who has worked with Kissinger for years exploded in the course of our interview. (Ronald Reagan was at the moment campaigning for President against the secretary of state, who, he said, was giving too much away to his friends the Russians.) But, the Kissinger aide argued, "Henry understands that to stand up to the Russians you can't go on an emotional jag. We are not going to get rid of the Soviet system, so we have to live with it."

The willing suspension of disbelief about ultimate goals has made it possible to modify the conspiracy theory which for twenty-five years had had a powerful influence on the conduct of American foreign policy. It was rational. It was overdue. Indeed, it can be argued that changing the official way of looking at the Soviet Union was an essential part of any successful strategy for containing Soviet power and maintaining American preeminence. Eschatological visions, anticommunist crusades were anachronistic and crippling. But, as we shall see, modernizing the official image of the enemy involved some domestic political costs.

Another new idea was something the press quickly called "linkage." Kissinger had written in a number of places that arms control was a political not a technical problem, that progress on cutting back on weapons depended upon political accommodation. These were not unconventional ideas. Most political theorists subscribed to the notion that arms were symptoms, not causes, of political insecurity. Years before, Dulles had challenged the Russians to show by their "deeds, not words" that they could be trusted. But the concept of orchestrating negotiations in one area to keep them in step with negotiations in other areas, while not unprecedented, had never been tried as an explicit national policy. After a few days in office Kissinger proposed to do just that.

He had hoped to do it quietly, by private diplomacy, making it clear to the Russians, who within hours of Nixon's conciliatory inaugural address had called for the start of the SALT talks, that he was "ready to move on a broad front" to achieve "the right balance of interests." But Nixon, who was fascinated with the idea of diplomatic barter, unveiled the "linkage" strategy at a press conference seven days after taking office. In answer to a question about when the arms talks would start he said: "It's a question of not only when but the context of those talks. What I want to do is to see to it that we have strategic arms talks in a way and at a time that will promote, if possible, progress on outstanding political problems at the same time—for example, on the problem of the Middle East and on other outstanding problems in which the United States and the Soviet Union, acting together, can serve the cause of peace."

Linkage was an idea that ruffled feathers in several places. (Within days of taking office Cyrus Vance, Kissinger's successor, announced its demise.) The Soviets, not surprisingly, thought it was a form of diplomatic extortion, and neither Kissinger's public statement on February 9, 1969, that it was "no attempt to blackmail" the Russians "into a disadvantageous settlement in order to give something in another area" nor frequent private sessions with Ambassador Dobrynin led to an apparent change of the Soviet view. "Henry took a lot of flak in those days," an aide recalls. "State wanted to extend credits to the Russians and sign an airplane agreement. The arms people wanted him to accept the SALT offer. Our European allies wanted Henry to accept the Russian proposal for convening a European security conference. There was even political pressure from Republicans to have a quick summit meeting with the Russians. After all, Kennedy had one." But Kissinger "deliberately stalled," as one of his close assistants put it, trying to fit the pieces of the U.S.-Soviet relationship into a coherent structure in which each would reinforce the other. How it worked we shall see.

What changes in Soviet thinking prepared the way for the Nixon-Brezhnev détente, the spirit of which, despite setbacks, still dominates U.S.-Soviet relationships? Boris Rabbot, formerly Scientific Secretary of the Soviet Academy of Sciences, worked closely with the vice-president of the academy, A. M. Rumyantsev, from 1965 to 1971 on the development of scientific and cultural contacts with the United States. These were critical years for the evolution of Soviet policy, and the academy played an important role in the first soundings of Soviet leadership on the ideas that became the basis of the U.S.-Soviet détente. Rabbot's inside view is confirmed by a number of other bits of evidence, but a word of caution is in order. In some ways the Soviet Union now is less of an enigma than when Stalin held absolute power. There is a much greater flow of information from Russia. But decentralization of power, the rise of bureaucratic fiefdoms in the military and elsewhere, the increasing complexity of the society, all conspire to make the Soviet Union today, as the French Kremlinologist Michel Tatu points out, more of a mystery in some ways than in Stalin's day. Rabbot himself says that it is more of a mystery than it needs to be because Western analysts still work with the model of Stalinist Russia and have not assimilated the enormous changes of the last ten years into their thinking. Nevertheless the contours of Soviet thinking on détente emerge rather clearly.

When Khrushchev was overthrown, just six months after his extravagant seventieth-birthday celebration in October 1964, the new leaders confronted the same massive problems that had led to their ebullient predecessor's downfall: military inferiority, dramatized by the humiliation of what the Soviets call the "October crisis" in the Caribbean; low agricultural productivity despite Khrushchev's ambitious schemes to cultivate the vast "virgin lands" of Siberia, which had necessitated a $250 million grain purchase in the United States (Nixon at the time thought the deal "harmed the cause of freedom. Why should we pull them out of their trouble and make communism look better?"); falling industrial productivity; increasing hostility of China; restiveness in Eastern Europe. Between 1964 and 1969 Russia was ruled by a troika, Brezhnev, Kosygin, and Podgorny, who moved cautiously in both domestic and foreign policy as each waited for one of their number to emerge as the supreme leader. The Soviets were slow to pursue the arms proposals of the Johnson administration (Vietnam was obviously an obstacle and the proposals were not very attractive), and they were cautious about advancing a new German policy. The invasion of Czechoslovakia symbolized Russia's moral weakness, not its strength. Soviet leaders were well aware of the price they would pay.

There were two great differences between Khrushchev's efforts in détente in the 1957–1964 period, Rabbot points out, and the efforts of his successors in the late 1960s. While the objectives were the same—to secure from the United States recognition of the Soviet Union as the second world power—the methods were different. Khrushchev genuinely wanted peaceful relations with the United States, but he hoped to compel the Americans to settle the outstanding issues—Berlin, Cuba, nuclear proliferation—on favorable terms by the pressures of crisis diplomacy. His successors thought that was much too dangerous and believed that building a more stable relationship at reduced levels of tension would better achieve that goal. Then, too, Khrushchev dealt in the illusions of power. Not only did he pretend to have missiles and technological superiority that did not exist but he preferred to deal with the gathering economic crisis within the Soviet Union by denying it and boasting about achievements that were never to take place in his time. His successors were bent on building the reality of power. This required not only spending much more than Khrushchev had been willing to spend on the military but also admitting the serious weaknesses that beset the Soviet economy. Stalin, Khrushchev said once, actually thought that every Soviet family had a chicken on the table every day. No one dared to discuss the economy at all until 1950, when it became clear even to Stalin that the continuing economic crisis could not be blamed on the devastation of war alone. Khrushchev's extravagant promises had not put chickens on the table either.

His successors were determined to make some economic reforms. Kosygin, the premier, wanted to modernize the Soviet planning system. Planning, he said in April 1965, "is not only an economic activity, as people often believe. It is the solving of social problems linked with the raising of people's standard of living . . . We have to free ourselves completely . . . from everything that used to tie down the planning officials and obliged them to draft plans otherwise than in accordance with the interests of the economy . . . In the course of analyzing many important problems, we often find ourselves prisoners of laws we ourselves have made, which should have been replaced long ago by new principles corresponding to the modern conditions that govern the development of production." It was as explicit a technocrat's brief against the stranglehold of party ideologists as finds public expression in the Soviet Union. It resulted in the limited industrial reform adopted at the September 1965 Plenum of the Central Committee. The authority and flexibility of plant managers were somewhat increased, but these unorthodox moves in the direction of decentralization were balanced by an increased role for the party in ideological matters. After a brief thaw a Stalinist campaign against ideological impurity in literature and the arts resumed. The dissident writers Sinyavsky and Daniel were arrested in the month in which the Plenum met. The dilemma of how to modernize the economy, catch up with the United States in missiles, increase consumer goods, and strengthen the authority of the party all at the same time, Rabbot says, led Soviet planners increasingly to reexamine the frozen relationship with the West.

Relations with the Chinese also took a dramatic turn as the new Soviet leaders took over. China had exploded an atomic bomb, and at the Ninth Party Congress in 1965 had elevated the dispute with the Soviet Union from a personal and ideological attack on Khrushchev to a denunciation of the Soviet state, against which the Chinese now made public territorial claims. While the Soviet leaders always hold open the possibility of patching up relations with China, Rabbot says, Lin Piao's speech at the party congress convinced the new Kremlin leadership that the struggle with China was a serious long-term security problem, and that too made détente with the United States look increasingly attractive. According to Maurice Couve de Murville, De Gaulle's foreign minister, Kosygin told him in 1966 that while China was "disquieting," his preoccupation was "to know what the game of the United States would be in the future. Indeed, the most alarming unknown factor was the possible Chinese-American connection." A working group within the Soviet leadership proposed a bigger Soviet role in the Vietnam settlement as a way of sharpening the conflict between America and China.

It was not merely increased awareness of problems, however, but also increased confidence that caused the new Soviet leaders to think positively about a process of increasing engagement with the United States. (The term "peaceful engagement," coined by Zbigniew Brzezinski, was gaining currency in the United States.) The confidence was born not only of their own missile buildup and a new merchant marine capable of delivering arms to distant places but also of a realization that the United States had made a major blunder in Indochina, with far-reaching repercussions for changing the balance of power in the world to the benefit of the Soviet Union. On top of all this was a new sophistication about the outside world. The rise of "think tanks" and study groups—the Institute for the Study of the United States, the Institute of World Economy and International Relations, study groups within the Academy of Sciences and in the Central Committee staff—has provided Soviet leaders with much more precise information about what is happening in the outside world and what it means. In the past the Soviet leaders have appeared as reluctant as their American counterparts to be drawn into serious negotiations, and probably for the same reason—fear of the unknown and concern about being entangled in a process they could not control. But by the late 1960s it seemed that they had little to lose by trying.

The process of détente began in Europe. The first country with which Khrushchev's successors sought a new relationship was France. In 1944 De Gaulle had visited Moscow and proposed a Franco-Soviet alliance (to be followed by Anglo-Soviet and Anglo-French alliances, and then only by a wider relationship, including the United States) for the purpose, as De Gaulle would later put it, of allowing France to play "an international role of the first rank." With the neighboring states of West Europe France would forge a third power bloc able to act as "the arbiter between the Soviet and Anglo-Saxon camps." It all came to nothing at the time. Stalin had once asked, "How many divisions has the Pope?" when it was suggested at a diplomatic conference that more deference be paid to His Holiness; in 1944 De Gaulle had a negligibly larger number. But in 1965, when Soviet Foreign Minister Andrei Gromyko visited the general in Paris, things were different. De Gaulle had power, not so much because of the French divisions or even the *force de frappe* but because of his unique position to use the politics of *grandeur* to dash American hopes for a U.S.-dominated Atlantic community. In February 1966 De Gaulle announced what he had been hinting for more than a year—France would leave NATO. All U.S. troops must leave France. In June he went to Moscow, where, according to Couve de Murville, Brezhnev broached the idea of a European security conference, from which the U.S. would be excluded. For De Gaulle the new relationship with the Soviets was to be the first stage of an entente, in the tradition of the Franco-Russian alliances of 1892 and 1935, which would lead to a "Europe from the Atlantic to the Urals." For the Soviets the détente with France meant a welcome increase of tensions in the West and a weakening of NATO.

The Johnson administration was dominated by such old-fashioned Atlanticists as Dean Rusk, for whom De Gaulle became an obsession second only to the North Vietnamese. Nixon took a different view. He admired the general and looked to him for lessons in *grandeur*. Besides, by the time Nixon came to office the damage had been done and De Gaulle's star had already set. (He never recovered from the upheavals of 1968, and he resigned early in 1969.)

But the action had shifted to Germany. During the years of the so-called Grand Coalition (1966–1969), when Willy Brandt was foreign minister, *Ostpolitik* and détente became for the first time respectable things to discuss, in large part because the French defection from NATO had put the whole Western anti-Soviet strategy into question. But no moves were made because the price—continued division of Germany and weakened ties with the United States—seemed too high. The dominant view in Washington and Bonn remained as Henry Kissinger had expressed it ten years earlier. "The Federal Republic would suffer a perhaps irreparable blow if its allies accepted its present frontiers as final—even to the extent of not pressing for reunification." But in the fall of 1969 the Social Democrats won a clear majority and Brandt took over as chancellor. In less than a year *Ostpolitik,* embodied in a Soviet-German treaty and a Polish-German treaty, became a reality. The border between East and West Germany and the Oder-Neisse Line dividing East Germany and Poland were given legal recognition. "Russia is inextricably woven into the history of Europe," Brandt declared in an address in Moscow in August 1970, "not only as an adversary and danger but also as a partner —historical, political, cultural, and economic."

These momentous changes in German foreign policy caused considerable disquiet in the Nixon administration. Kissinger did not share the fear that pervaded the State Department in the 1950s that, frustrated by the failure to win reunification, West Germany would turn east and make a deal with the Soviet Union, as the Weimar Republic had done briefly at Rapallo. Indeed, he believed that an initiative on the German borders and a Berlin settlement were overdue, but he was nervous about Brandt, whom he thought somewhat naïve, and was fearful that the German negotiations, once they started, would race ahead of the other issues on which he was seeking to engage the Soviets. In other words, if the Germans controlled the negotiations, the results would be less favorable for the West because linkage would not be possible. Kissinger was worried that the German Social Democrats would give away too much and thereby divide and weaken their own country. In Berlin, unlike at the SALT talks or in economic relations, the Soviets held almost all the cards. But Brandt was not consulting the United States on the details. In April 1970 Kissinger sent word to Brandt to "wait for us" in his approaches to the Russians. (In August 1970, the month Brandt signed the protocol on the Oder-Neisse Line, Kissinger stated in a press backgrounder that the United States had not yet formulated a policy on Berlin.)

Helmut Sonnenfeldt complains that the charge made against Kissinger in the 1976 campaign that he ignored the European allies in the pursuit of détente was unfair. Indeed, for a while, he says, it was the Germans who were ignoring the Americans. The Germans heard Nixon say publicly in March 1969 that he was ready to negotiate on Berlin, and they did not want to wait until a U.S.-Soviet deal had been consummated. But the speed of the German initiative forced Kissinger's hand. It was precisely what Soviet planners had hoped when they began their German initiative in the late 1960s.

The Berlin issue, over which the world had been on the brink of war in the summer of 1961, was swept up in the rush of other events. At the Twenty-fourth Party Congress in early 1971 Leonid Brezhnev made a strong public commitment to détente with the United States, for the first time staking his prestige as the emerging leader—the pretense of "collective leadership" was fading fast—on "peaceful entanglement" with the United States. When the private Kissinger-Dobrynin talks resumed in April, the Soviet ambassador, who had been promoted at the Party Congress to a full member of the Central Committee, was prepared to bargain. On May 20, 1971, a breakthrough in the SALT negotiations was announced.

The Soviets had made one major concession, the Americans another. The Soviets had agreed to ignore the U.S. "forward based systems," aircraft carriers, short-range planes operating from bases near the Soviet Union—all capable of landing nuclear weapons on Soviet soil. Some estimates indicate that as many as 30,000 of these weapons, many as large as or larger than the Hiroshima bomb, could strike Soviet territory.

The United States, for its part, dropped its demand that both sides be limited to an equal number of offensive long-range missiles and in effect conceded to the Soviets a 3–2 edge on ICBMs. In the private discussions SALT and Berlin issues were traded off against each other. When the quadripartite agreement on Berlin was signed on September 3, 1971, the Soviets had retreated on one major point. They dropped their argument that only the East Germans had the authority to guarantee the access to Berlin and they assumed the responsibility themselves.

Between the start of the serious "back-channel" negotiations, in the jargon of the Kissinger White House, and the signing of the agreement a momentous event had intervened—Kissinger's trip to China. Soviet policy, by being heavy-handed, had inadvertently created the very conditions for the U.S.-Chinese détente that Nixon and Kissinger had sought as an instrument to make the Soviets a "more manageable adversary." In March 1969 fighting broke out on Damansky Island (the Chinese call it Chenpao Island) in the Ussuri River, which flows between Manchuria and the Maritime Province of the Soviet Far East. In the following summer further clashes occurred in the Amur River and on the boundary of Sinkiang Province. Negotiations to resolve the three-centuries-old border dispute that had sparked the fighting quickly stalled.

Soon thereafter the Soviets, presumably to intimidate the Chinese, began a coordinated campaign to raise the specter of a Soviet preemptive strike on the Chinese nuclear force—a strategy, it will be recalled, that had been briefly considered and rejected by the United States in the Rusk era. Victor Louis, a well-known KGB operative who plants stories in the Western press which the Soviet Government wishes to circulate, wrote a piece for the London *Evening News* in which he reported that the Soviet Union was considering a surprise nuclear attack on China. Soviet diplomats began hinting the same thing privately to Americans whom they met. The effect of course was to alarm China and cause her to turn more quickly to the United States. This in turn made the Russians even more interested in the U.S.-Soviet détente.

CHAPTER 3
Détente: What It Is

When Soviet officials are asked to define "détente," they usually say that the word describes sixty-odd agreements covering a wide variety of subjects from nuclear weapons to the avoidance of accidents at sea to cooperation for developing new techniques for heart surgery. The two centerpieces in the structure are the SALT agreements and the Berlin accord. The latter agreement has been singled out by critics of détente as the symbol of the "one-way street" down which a naïve America is supposedly being led. Kissinger's critics are right in noting that the Berlin accord and the American blessing of Brandt's *Ostpolitik* gave the Soviets what they always wanted—recognition of East Germany and the fruits of their World War II victories, for which little was received in return. But the issues had been settled on the battlefield thirty years before, and it was statesmanlike to stop the pretense that they hadn't. The agreement, according to one of Kissinger's top aides who helped draft it, was a "Band-Aid," but it involved several advantages for the United States and West Berlin. It defused the crisis and deprived the Soviets of an issue—access to Berlin —on which the only American recourse was to threaten war. The siege atmosphere, which was beginning to take its toll in West Berlin, lifted. Several thousand East Germans have emigrated to West Germany. Travel to West Berlin is freer. Telephone communications have been restored. (Before the agreement, calls from one part of the city to the other were routed through Copenhagen and Moscow.) West Berlin is still a city with a superannuated and a declining population facing an uncertain future, but it is better off than in its heroic days when John F. Kennedy declared "Ich bin ein Berliner" on his way back to Washington.

The story of the SALT talks has been told in fascinating detail in John Newhouse's *Cold Dawn*. Besides the modest agreements that they produced, the negotiations yielded a number of important insights into the Soviet system for the American elite. We can only guess that the Soviet leaders derived similar benefits.

During the SALT talks it became clear that Soviet generals were sometimes uninformed about their own weapons systems and extremely wary about even discussing Soviet forces. The U.S. generals who participated in the negotiations express irritation that only U.S. data on Soviet systems is used as a basis of discussion and only U.S. code names for Soviet airplanes ("Bison," "Backfire," etc.) are mentioned at the negotiating table, since the Soviets' own designations are kept secret. Yet Brezhnev himself was much more forthcoming. According to one of Kissinger's aides who was present at the Moscow summit, he volunteered information—which turned out to be accurate—about a new weapons system that U.S. intelligence had not believed existed. He also told Kissinger about some U.S. weapons tests of which the national security adviser had been unaware.

The twice weekly SALT negotiations are ritualistic. The Soviets read their statements. Except when "conceptual breakthroughs," as Kissinger calls them, occur at higher levels, there is little give and take. "The Soviets," one member of the U.S. delegation says, "like us to take extreme positions so that they can bargain us down."

Members of the two delegations have come to know one another after years of biweekly meetings. They play golf and tennis together on occasion and exchange dinner invitations. Mostly they study one another. The American delegation has a dossier on each of their counterparts, as, presumably, the Soviets do also. Members of the U.S. team are particularly fascinated with Vladimir Semonov, the ranking Soviet negotiator (a cultured man who reads philosophy, knows the Bible better than the Americans, and loves ballet). Semonov knew Stalin and worked under Beria. His two immediate superiors were executed in Stalin's purges. "We keep wondering," one member of the delegation put it, "why did he survive?"

The third centerpiece of détente is the statement of basic principles that Nixon and Brezhnev signed in 1972 and Kissinger called a "road map" for détente. It is a list of ground rules for coexistence expressed in diplomatically vague language. The most important provision is an obligation to "consult" each other concerning "the development of situations capable of causing a dangerous exacerbation of their relations." The two powers have "a special responsibility . . . to do everything in their power so that conflicts or situations will not arise which would serve to increase international tensions." This statement has been the focus of controversy. Despite its general nature it proposes to provide criteria for judging whether détente is working.

Critics like Senator Henry Jackson, the editors of *Fortune,* and such skeptical students of Soviet affairs as Robert Conquest, Brian Crozier, Leopold Labedz, Richard Pipes, and Leonard Schapiro contend that the Soviets in the Middle East and in Angola have violated the letter and the spirit of this accord. The most egregious example, they say, is the Soviet failure either to notify the United States of the impending Egyptian attack on Israel that began on October 6, 1973, or to stop it. Kissinger's top aides say that it is completely unrealistic to have expected either initiative from the Soviets.

On October 1 the Soviet ambassador was summoned by President Sadat and told that an attack might be launched by the Egyptians in the near future. The date was kept secret not only for security reasons but also for fear that the Russians might try to stop the attack. Indeed, as Mohammed Heikel, then an adviser to Sadat, puts it, it was the fear that "détente will set conditions for the Middle East problem . . . and impose itself on us" that convinced Sadat the 1973 war "was Egypt's last chance." Three days later the Soviet ambassador delivered to Sadat an urgent request from Brezhnev that Russian civilian advisers and their families be immediately evacuated. They left about twenty-four hours before the first intelligence reports reached Moshe Dayan, the Israeli defense minister, that the Egyptian attack was imminent.

"You have been very quick about your civilians," Sadat said to the Soviet ambassador, "but not so quick about the stuff I asked for"— meaning the military supplies that the Soviets had promised and had so far failed to deliver. During the years between Israel's attack on Egypt in 1967 and Egypt's attack on Israel in 1973 Soviet-Egyptian relations were mercurial and often stormy. The Soviets had suffered a loss of prestige too in the Six-Day War because Nasser had been a client since the late 1950s, and they offered to send new weapons, but not the most modern weapons the Egyptians wanted. (The Soviets did not disguise their contempt for the Egyptian Army. "What do you need more arms for," Marshal Matvei Zakharov taunted Nasser's officers, "to deliver them to the Israelis too?") In 1970 Nasser asked for and received advanced surface-to-air missiles and Soviet technician crews to man them. The next year the Soviets signed a fifteen-year friendship treaty with Anwar Sadat, who had succeeded as

Egyptian president. But tensions mounted. The Soviets delivered fewer and less modern reconnaissance planes than they had promised (the MIG-21 instead of the MIG-23), and never any bombers. They infuriated the Egyptians by asking for free access to Egyptian ports and permanent staging and overflight rights at Egyptian airfields, and were denied them. Pro-Soviet politicians were arrested. On July 18, 1872, Sadat ordered all Soviet technicians and advisers out of the country. Soviet arms shipments increased dramatically, but relations cooled. Curiously, the more arms the Soviets delivered, the less influence they seemed to have. The Egyptians were fearful that Brezhnev would try to use their dependence on Soviet arms to keep them from starting a war that could jeopardize détente, but the Russians never had that power. Once their prestige was so heavily invested in the Egyptian cause, they had no choice but to supply arms to keep Egypt from being defeated. But in demonstrating their unwillingness to give enough arms to make her victorious they undercut their own influence in the region. Today, as a leading Soviet diplomat put it recently, "We are out."

Had the Soviets told the United States about the attack twenty-four hours before it occurred—which was the first time they knew the exact date—a high White House aide privately admits that American officials would have passed on the information to Golda Meir. The Russians would have done exactly the same had the United States given them advance warning of an Israeli attack, which is why, the aide explains, the United States never would honor the obligation to "consult."

The U.S.-Soviet confrontation in Angola, critics argue, is proof that détente doesn't work. Between March 1975 and February 1976, 11,000 Cuban combat troops and $300 million in Soviet military equipment were introduced into Angola, resulting in a victory for the MPLA, the Soviet-backed faction in the struggle to take power from the Portuguese. Warning that "this type of action will not be tolerated again," Kissinger canceled meetings of various joint commissions that were to have planned the next stages in U.S.-Soviet cooperation and approved a stepped-up program of military aid to Africa. But he did not exercise leverage by delaying the SALT talks or suspending the large grain sales to the U.S.S.R. Brezhnev's public reply came a few weeks later. "Détente," the Chairman declared at the Twenty-fifth Soviet Communist Party Congress, "does not in the slightest abolish, and cannot abolish or alter, the laws of the class struggle . . . No one should expect that because of détente Communists will reconcile themselves with capitalist exploitation or that monopolists become followers of the revolution . . . We make no secret of the fact that we see détente as the way to create more favorable conditions for peaceful socialist and communist construction. This only confirms that socialism and peace are indissoluble." Privately, Brezhnev made a point of reassuring the Americans that Angola was a special situation and not likely to be repeated.

The Angola episode dramatized the contradictions inherent in the new relationship of the superpowers. Since the Cuban missile crisis there has been a conscious effort by the strategists in Moscow as well as in Washington to avoid direct confrontations. In Portugal the Soviets, while continuing to give covert financial support to the Portuguese Communist party, did not directly oppose the considerable diplomatic and covert activities of the United States and West European governments that defeated the leftist forces there. The United States has been somewhat more cautious in recent years about avoiding direct confrontations. But on at least two occasions since the Cuban missile crisis the United States has demonstrated that it is prepared to take that risk in order to advance some other objective. One such occasion was on February 1965, when the first aerial bombardment of North Vietnam was ordered. "Your daddy may have started World War III," Lyndon Johnson told his daughter. Another was the 1972 bombing and mining of Haiphong Harbor, which was filled with Soviet ships. The Soviet Union has made it clear many times that it does not underwrite revolutions beyond the reach of territory controlled by the Soviet Army. But in Angola there were at least three factors that made the attempt irresistible. One was the presence of the Chinese. Another was the presence of the South Africans. A third was the fact that the United States, fresh from the defeat in Vietnam, was hobbled by domestic forces from matching the Soviet commitment. To a considerable extent Soviet opportunity was the child of American blunder.

When the armed forces in Portugal overthrew the government of Salazar's successor in April 1974, it was apparent that the long independence war in Portuguese Africa (Angola, Guinea-Bissau, Mozambique) would soon come to an end. In Angola three separate insurgent groups were carrying on the struggle, sometimes with one another as much as with the Portuguese. Each had received outside assistance for many years. The splits among them were as much ethnic as political, and the Portuguese had been encouraging them in traditional colonial fashion. The FNLA (National Front for the Liberation of Angola) had its support in the Bakongo tribe in the north. Its leader was Holden Roberto, an émigré politician who set up a secure base in Zaire, financed by several millions of dollars from the CIA that were funneled through the president of Zaire. (In 1969, in a move reflecting Kissinger's diminished interest in Africa at the time, payments to Roberto were reduced to a $10,000 retainer.) From 1973 on, the Chinese also supported Roberto, and sent him a 120-man training mission under the command of a major general from Peking. By late 1974 he was doing very well on the military front.

A second group, UNITA (United Union for the Total Independence of Angola), split from FNLA in 1964. It was headed by Jonas Savimbi, a Swiss-educated former assistant of Roberto, and had its ethnic base in the much larger Ovimbundu tribe, in the central plateau of Angola. Savimbi preached self-reliance, quoting Mao on how revolutions should be made with the guns of the enemy, but he took a few guns from the Chinese too.

The faction which eventually emerged victorious was the MPLA (Popular Movement for the Liberation of Angola), which drew its tribal support from the Mbundu people concentrated around Luanda, and its ideology from the Portuguese left. Agostinho Neto, the leader, is a Portuguese-educated physician with a Portuguese wife. For more than a decade before his victory he had been receiving Soviet and East European training and arms in modest amounts.

As John A. Marcum, provost of the University of California at Santa Cruz and the author of *The Angolan Revolution,* points out, "The FNLA entered the 1975 power struggle for control of independent Angola from a position of military but not political strength." Roberto had spent most of his years of struggle in exile. He had a reputation, publicly handed to him by the president of Guinea, Sekou Touré, of being a CIA agent, and his movement had a narrow tribal base. But he had arms. In mid-1974 the Chinese stepped up their support.

In two respects the United States repeated its Vietnam experience in Angola. In January 1975 the "40 Committee" of the National Security Council authorized covert support for Roberto of $300,000, because, as Marcum says, it was "the movement with the largest army and the one most disposed to follow a military rather than a political strategy." Once again the illusion that weapons and money could overcome lack of political support or political skill became the base for building disastrous policies.

The second illusion borrowed from the Vietnam War was to invest the local struggle in Angola with global significance. "Vietnam isn't important in itself," the Johnson administration used to say. "It just happens to be the focus of the worldwide struggle with Communism." So also in Angola the primary American concern was not what would happen to Angola but whether the Soviet Union would become "a dominant influence in south-central Africa" and would "threaten the stability of the area." Rather than deciding what American security interests were involved in Angola and what difference it would make which faction won, the United States chose sides. Between July and December 1975 the United States secretly (to avoid "a public confrontation" with Congress, State Department officials said) sent between $30 million and $50 million in military equipment into the African bush to Roberto's and Savimbi's forces. Marcum's analysis of how all this was likely to affect détente is instructive:

> Given the circumstances, American action and reaction seemed almost designed to provoke the Russians into seeking maximum advantage. Because the Soviet Union's outreach as a superpower is more military than economic, and because its capacity to intervene is essentially unconstrained by democratic accountability, there might have been every reason to conclude that the Soviets would enjoy an advantage in the event of an Angola war by proxy. One would have thought that the President and Secretary of State would have perceived, as the Soviet leadership must have, that an American public chastened and disillusioned by a lost war in Vietnam would not tolerate even a very modest involvement in another distant, unfathomable, civil conflict.

In August, Cuban technicians and military instructors began to arrive in greater numbers in Angola. Since 1965, when Che Guevara was in the Congo, Cubans have been training guerrillas, teachers, and doctors in Angola, Guinea-Bissau, and Mozambique. Two hundred Cubans fought in the long independence war in Guinea-Bissau and some were killed or captured by the Portuguese. In late October, South Africa intervened from the south with a column of 1,200 South African regulars which also included troops from Zaire and European mercenaries. By November 11, the day the Portuguese had agreed to leave Angola, the South African force had captured several towns on the coast, in the central area, and on the Zambian border. It appeared as though the de facto alliance of U.S. money and arms and South African military power would defeat the MPLA. At this point Soviet arms shipments became massive (22 transport planes began landing tanks and rockets) and Cuban combat troops arrived in strength to take over the fighting at the front.

Within weeks the tide of battle had turned. In December, Kissinger's request for "trivial sums" for covert aid to bolster the FNLA-UNITA forces (some "tens of million of dollars" were needed, the secretary of state said) was turned down in the Senate by a vote of 54 to 22. African states, including Nigeria and Tanzania, which had been critical of Soviet intervention in Africa, now rallied to the MPLA because of the South African intervention on the other side. The Chinese discreetly withdrew. By February the MPLA had won.

Despite the obligations of the two big powers to consult with each other to avoid confrontations, there was no communication at crucial moments of the crisis. The United States did not, as Marcum points out, try preventive diplomacy. "Moscow was left to draw its own conclusions about American intentions." One FNLA leader said that the United States banged its fist on the table and the Russians took them seriously and sent aid which the Americans couldn't match.

Just as the presidential election campaign was getting under way, the détente had become more vulnerable than ever. The most humiliating aspect of the operation for the administration was the use of the Cuban troops. The revolution ninety miles away that had survived invasions, assassination attempts, and a fifteen-year embargo had played a crucial role in handing the United States a major diplomatic defeat halfway around the world. The sudden appearance of Cuban combat troops also underscored the reality that the Soviets were now in a position to fight proxy wars in distant places, although it was unclear whether the Cuban troops were instruments of Soviet policy or were acting out their own revolutionary agenda. While he publicly talked of the "Soviet intervention" in Angola and called Cuba a "client state," Kissinger told reporters he rejected the theory that "Castro had been forced by Soviet pressure to send the troops." "I believe the Cubans went in there with flags flying." If so, then the 1975 episode in Angola is similar to the 1973 Middle East war in one crucial aspect. In neither case was the Soviet Union in control of events. In both cases the price of withholding aid was more than the Soviets could afford to pay.

At the 1972 Moscow summit, John Newhouse tells us, all sorts of agreements popped up like crocuses. Several were agreements on scientific and technical cooperation. Further agreements were concluded at the two subsequent summits in 1973 and 1974. In all, there are eleven of them. The most dramatic is the space agreement under which the Apollo-Soyuz television spectacular in space was produced in July 1975. Joint U.S.-Soviet rescue missions for future manned flights that get into trouble are being planned. One of the most successful has been the Agreement on Cooperation in Medical Science and Public Health, under which joint laboratory and clinical research on cancer and cardiovascular diseases is being conducted and scientists, equipment, information, and biological specimens are being exchanged. Therapeutic agents for controlling cancer used in the two countries are being compared biochemically in U.S. and Soviet laboratories. An artificial-heart agreement was signed in 1974, under which the two countries are collaborating on plans for "total heart replacement." Under the Agreement for Cooperation in Peaceful Uses of Atomic Energy, U.S. scientists now have access to Soviet large-scale breeder reactor technology, which is more advanced than the state of the art in the United States. In transportation there is joint work on civil aviation landing systems. Little has been done in housing, but plans are progressing for joint research on "construction in areas of extreme climatic conditions." There is an energy agreement as well under which U.S. magnetohydrodynamics experts are assisting at a Soviet pilot power project. (Plans for an intergovernmental project on underground coal gasification have proved impractical because a private U.S. firm purchased the Soviet technology in this area.) U.S. and Soviet scientists have begun exploring the ocean floor together. Soviet citizens act as cochief scientists on expeditions of the *Glomar Challenger,* the oceanic exploration vessel. Earthquakes, pollution, and other environmental problems are also areas of joint research.

The purpose of these agreements on science and technology, Acting Assistant Secretary of State Myron B. Kratzer has testified, "is to foster restraint and cooperation with the Soviet Union across a broad spectrum of our relations." Such cooperation, he says, "is an effective means of developing normal relations and reducing tensions." Hundreds of Soviet scientists, scholars, and others, including "young political leaders," come to the United States each year, and hundreds of Americans visit the Soviet Union. Historians and archivists are beginning to cooperate on joint research on archival materials. According to Dr. Frederick Starr of the Kennan Institute, the Soviets now show interest in exchanging archival materials even on the cold-war period. A number of cultural exchange projects have stalled, not for lack of Soviet cooperation but for lack of American money.

What is the purpose of all these agreements? What are the two societies getting out of them? It is an attractive idea that technicians and scholars from the two giant adversaries cooperate on the common problems of humanity that dwarf the differences between them. Fighting cancer, environmental pollution, and earthquakes side by side rather than fighting each other is eminently rational. Jointly probing some of the mysteries of the universe is a much more wholesome activity than plotting new and exquisite forms of destruction. But the layer of cooperation now being superimposed upon the politico-military competition is thin. Soviet diplomats like to define détente in quantitative terms. "We have eleven technical agreements, and so many arms-control agreements," and so forth. But as John Thomas of the National Science Foundation, who monitors many of the scientific and technical agreements, points out, cooperation must be measured primarily in qualitative terms. Numbers give a clue, to be sure. Although we have had some form of scientific cooperation with the Soviet Union since 1958, the number of Soviet scientists who visit the United States annually is still fewer than a thousand. Scientific cooperation with much smaller countries is on a much grander scale. But the real question is what fundamental long-term changes in the relationship will result.

The State Department sees the cultural, scientific, and technical cooperation program as helping to build the web of entanglements that will keep the two powers at peace. The contact between the two scientific elites is considered valuable in itself. The symbolism is important. For the Soviet Union there is a clearly expressed interest in using these programs for increased access to technology. Although, as we shall see, the major source of American technology for the Soviets is commercial deals, the scientific exchanges are also useful for them. Administration spokesmen are careful to point out that the flow of information under the cooperation agreements is a two-way street. Indeed, particularly in theoretical research, the Soviets are ahead in a number of fields, and American scientists are eager to grasp the opportunity to learn from them. As a general rule, John Thomas says, the Soviets are less likely to be ahead of their U.S. counterparts in applied technology, though there are some areas, such as coal gasification, in which American technologists have much to learn from them.

American officials make no secret of the fact that they hope increased scientific and technical contact will help to produce long-term changes in Soviet society by encouraging more openness and freedom and less ideological control by the party. Soviet officials by their actions make no secret of their wish to minimize those very consequences. The political reliability of any scientist who is a candidate to make a research trip abroad or even to attend a conference is the first consideration. Each Soviet research institute has an official whose job is to make sure that none of the staff will do anything to embarrass the regime. A scientist applying for a visa to travel abroad in the interest of his work must submit his *characteristika,* a lengthy and elaborate form much like an application for a top-secret security clearance in the United States, on the basis of which party officials decide whether it is safe to let him go. The agreements with the United States now legitimize requests of scientists to travel abroad, but they also legitimize the control over the process by "competent authorities."

The distrust of the intelligentsia by the rulers of the Soviet Union is one of the contradictions that bedevil the system. The scientific, technical, and cultural elite, the leaders know, hold the key to expanded Soviet power. Yet the loyalty to the regime of the most privileged strata of the society is increasingly doubted. Khrushchev's memoirs offer a glimpse of the curious suspicion the top party bureaucrats reserve for the most distinguished Soviet citizens. Khrushchev personally decided to let the celebrated pianist Sviatoslav Richter travel abroad after ascertaining that his relations with his mother in West Germany were "cool." "Naturally it would be a shame to lose such a great muscian," he recalls telling his colleagues in the Kremlin, "but we simply can't mistrust everybody and suspect everybody of being a traitor. He may very well come back after all, and that would be good propaganda for our culture." The underlying assumption of dis-loyalty causes considerable unhappiness among the scientific elite, who range from such a man as Sakharov, with a fierce ideological commitment to intellectual freedom, to apolitical technicians who on a personal level resent being mistrusted and watched. The scientific exchange, limited as it has been, has helped Soviet scientists to realize what they have missed— the professional enrichment of being an active part of an international scientific community. It has helped, U.S. officials think, to create some vested interests within the Soviet Union in the preservation of the minimum international political conditions for continuing contacts. How the Soviet regime will deal with the scientific elite, an indispensable source of power but also a growing source of instability, will have great influence on what kind of society the Soviet Union will be in the year 2000.

For the Soviets, therefore, exchange agreements have costs as well as benefits. They are neither one-way streets, as the critics of détente like to say, nor two-way streets, as the defenders reply. Such agreements are more like an interconnecting network of avenues that lead in many un-certain directions. This is especially true of the Helsinki Agreement, one of the most publicized and controversial milestones on the road to détente. The Conference on Security and Cooperation in Europe at which the Helsinki Final Act (a diplomatic term of art implying an agreement of a political rather than legal nature) was signed on August 1, 1975, is the culmination of twenty years of Soviet diplomatic efforts. The Helsinki agreements were a special target in the 1976 presidential campaign, attacked by Ronald Reagan in the primaries and by Democrats in the general election as a one-sided affair. The Soviets had wanted such a conference for a long time to symbolize the general acceptance by the United States and West Europe of the division of Germany and the status of Eastern Europe. They had also hoped that such a conference would detach the United States from Europe. "There can be no doubt," the Warsaw Pact nations declared at Bucharest in 1966, "that the aims of the U.S. policy in Europe have nothing in common with the vital interests of the European peoples and the tasks of European security." What they got, despite an esoteric legal formula adopted at West German insistence, which is supposed to hold out some hope of peaceful readjustment of frontiers, is a document that everyone takes to be an affirmation of present borders and a legitimization of the status quo in Europe. It is in effect a multilateral reaffirmation of the agreements on Berlin and Germany and is one-sided in exactly the same way. The Soviets did not succeed in using the security conference to invite the United States out of Europe. What Brezhnev paid for the extravagant show produced at Helsinki were some political commitments on human rights that have already proved to be embarrassing. Basket Three, in the peculiar jargon of the agreements, calls for increased human contacts, including "reunification of families . . . travel for personal or professional reasons, improvement for conditions of tourism . . . meetings among young people, sports." It also provides for increased flow of information of all kinds . . . including improvement of the circulation and access to and exchange of oral, filmed and broadcast information and improvement of working conditions for journalists, co-operation and exchanges in the field of culture . . . and in educational fields. The language is diplomatically vague. There is much talk of taking "appropriate measures" and no talk of enforcement, but, as the President's first report on the Helsinki Agreement states, the principle is now established that "the daily situation of individual Europeans and improvement in broader political relationships between states" are linked. For the first time there is a basis for arguing that inquiries into these matters from abroad are not necessarily "intervention in internal Soviet affairs," which is the classic legal formula for embodying Stalin's dictum about capitalist snouts staying out of socialist gardens.

Basket One is primarily a set of general declarations, including a broad one on respect for human rights. There is relatively little to be implemented beyond certain "confidence-building measures," such as the obligation of NATO and Warsaw Pact countries to notify each other in advance of maneuvers involving 25,000 men or more. Countries holding such maneuvers are encouraged to invite observers. The agreement on advance notice has been observed on all sides, and some NATO and neutral observers have attended the Warsaw Pact military exercises, but neither the Soviets nor their allies have accepted invitations to attend West German, British, or Norwegian maneuvers.

Basket Two calls for increased cooperation in economics, science, and technology. Progress, according to President Ford's report, has been modest. The Soviets proposed an agreement to establish relations between the European community and the Council for Economic Mutual Assistance, but the idea of linking the economic organizations of the two halves of Europe has not, as the President's report points out, "generated much enthusiasm in the West." There has been little advance in economic statistics coming from the U.S.S.R. since the Helsinki Agreement despite the general commitment to improve economic and commercial information. Statistics from some of the other Warsaw Pact countries are much better.

Basket Three is about the international movement of people and ideas. It is vague because the Soviets resisted clearer language at Helsinki. It is controversial because it touches the most profound ideological differences that divide the liberal industrial state from state socialism. Capitalism is rooted in individualism, Soviet socialism in collective loyalty. The American constitutional system enshrines fundamental procedural rights such as freedom of speech, assembly, and religion. With these rights anyone is free —in theory if not always in practice—to acquire everything needed for a decent life—food, housing, medical care, a job. Without these rights life is not worth living. The essential promises the Soviet system makes to its citizens are substantive rights—minimum diet, minimum education for all, minimum health care, a guaranteed job—and the system in the present era does a relatively good job of delivering on these promises. The excesses of Stalinism are deplored and "socialist legality" is encouraged as a concept. But the party, not the individual, is firmly in charge of deciding how much procedural freedom—the right to speak, to think out loud, the right to assemble, to travel—is compatible with the substantive goals of the system.

Discussions of human rights in the Soviet Union tend to ignore the continuing impact of Russian history. The tradition of freedom is limited.

Russia has for centuries been an apolitical society mobilized from the top. Such discussions also ignore the practical difficulties Soviet leaders have in permitting alternative ideas to circulate freely in a depoliticized society for which the planning is done in the Kremlin and the source of political legitimacy is a monolithic party. Western critics tend to focus on those who are most obviously hurt by such a system—intellectuals, artists, and scientists, for whom procedural freedoms are essential to their craft and to their life—and to ignore the fact that the vast majority of Soviet citizens would probably choose substantive freedoms over procedural freedoms if they were forced to opt for one or the other.

Observations of this sort are sometimes offered as apologies for the outrageous behavior of Soviet officials toward their own citizens, as if there were no alternative to repression. But as Sakharov writes, the survival of the Soviet Union requires the spread of procedural freedoms, for without them the substantive rights cannot be the basis of civilization, only bare existence. The dissidents argue that the Soviet leaders cannot have a détente with the United States in any lasting or fundamental sense until they have a détente with the Soviet people. But that implies some basic changes in the Soviet system.

What influence have the Helsinki agreements had on the system? As far as official behavior is concerned, not much. At Helsinki the Soviets resisted the notion that emigration is a fundamental human right, but they did agree to facilitate emigration for the purpose of reuniting families. In 1975, 1,162 exit visas for the United States were given for this purpose. In the first six months of 1976, 1,303 such visas were issued. (Six years ago the number was 230.) Jewish emigration is not covered by the agreement. Since 1970, Jews have been allowed to leave the Soviet Union in greater numbers, but two months after the Moscow summit the Soviets imposed an "education tax" (based on years of schooling), which amounted in some cases to as much as a $25,000 fee for leaving. Under U.S. pressure the tax was removed, and as many as 35,000 Jews left the Soviet Union in 1973. In reaction to the Jackson Amendment, an attempt to link the granting of most-favored-nation status and credits to a Soviet agreement to allow the emigration of 60,000 Jews a year, the Soviets sharply curtailed Jewish emigration in 1974 and 1975. Shortly before the Carter administration took office the official number rose slightly.

Nor does the spirit of Helsinki appear to have penetrated widely within the Soviet Union. Vladimir Bukovsky, the prominent dissident who was exchanged for the Chilean communist leader Luis Corvalan, believes that Soviet prisons have become worse since the accords were signed. Alfred

Friendly, Jr., of the staff of the special executive-legislative commission set up to monitor compliance, sees a mixed picture. Throughout Eastern Europe more people are asking to emigrate, using Helsinki language as the basis for their petitions. Jews in the Soviet Union are still harassed when they apply for emigration. (It also appears that disillusioning reports of life in Israel have cooled some of the interest in emigration.) The authorities who ran a bulldozer over an avant-garde art exhibit in late 1974 were disciplined, and permission for what Friendly calls "the first Russian Woodstock" was given. But attacks on religious believers have been stepped up—especially on Lithuanian Catholics, Pentecostals, Jehovah's Witnesses, and Baptists. Teachers are harassed and private Sunday schools are broken up. Antireligious zeal varies widely in different parts of the country. Indeed, the whole pattern of repression is erratic and seems to be more a matter of local improvisation than enforcement of a monolithic party line. Reporting from Moscow for the Washington *Post* Peter Osnos gives an account of the variety of official reactions to dissident activities, from beatings of Jewish protesters to toleration of such *"nekulturniy"* behavior as wearing large stars of David in front of the Central Committee. A famous intellectual successfully scared off the KGB agents who had come to seize some more of his books by demanding to be arrested. A committee of dissidents to monitor Soviet compliance with the Helsinki agreements headed by Yuri Orlov was continually harassed but tolerated for months until Orlov's arrest in February 1977. A few years ago official reaction would have been quicker and surer and inevitably resulted in a long exile in Siberia. But authorities now face a dilemma. As a young "refusednik" told Osnos, Russia is now restrained by its own ambitions. If there were more arrests, "can you imagine the uproar in the West?" Yet a few days later in apparent response to the Carter administration's strong statement of its concern with human rights in the U.S.S.R., prominent dissidents including Alexander I. Ginsburg and Yuri Orlov were arrested. Dissidents in the Soviet Union had charged Kissinger with encouraging repression in the Soviet Union by making it clear to the Kremlin that, as in Iran, Indonesia, Brazil, and other places where American vital interests are at stake, the United States will avert its eyes, and they applauded the Carter administration's more forceful stance.

Anyone with ideas of his own who wishes to remain aloof from the "ideological struggle" or sees it in different terms from the party is a potential target of repression. Within the dissident movement are several distinct strains, ranging from the reactionary mysticism of Solzhenitsyn to the Leninism of Roy Medvedev, who wants the revolution to rediscover its roots. Andrei Sakharov is the most prominent representative of the constitutionalists, a group of scientists, writers, and intellectuals who accept the system but who insist that the impressive-sounding civil liberties provisions of the Soviet Constitution be observed. The movement started in December of 1965 when the fall of Khrushchev, who in his own way was the first prominent dissident, inspired fear of a return to Stalinism. A demonstration was held on Red Square, in which Pavel Litvinov, the grandson of the former commissar of foreign affairs, took part. To Soviet officialdom, Friendly points out, flaunting ideas of your own is a form of indecent exposure meriting swift dispatch to a mental hospital. The repressive use of mental hospitals is an Orwellian horror story, but Soviet officials seem to have little trouble equating certain kinds of dissent with madness.

The constitutionalists organized around the issue of an open trial for the dissidents under the slogan "Respect the Constitution." In the late 1960s a number of other prominent scientists joined Sakharov, but under pressure they moved back into official respectability, and some formerly overt sympathizers with the movement still hold high government and university positions. In 1968 repression in the Soviet Union became more severe in the aftermath of the brief life and death of "socialism with a human face" in Dubcek's Prague. Two *samizdat* publications, *The Chronicle of Current Events* and *Social Problems,* began to circulate and, except for an interruption of 17 months in 1972 and 1973, have continued to appear ever since. Sakharov won world attention by publishing parts of his extraordinary essay "Progress, Coexistence and Intellectual Freedom" in *The New York Times* in July 1968. From that moment the continuing battle between Soviet intellectuals and the authorities was joined. Dissidents now talked freely to Western correspondents—Edward Kline, a New York businessman who publishes *samizdat* writings in the U.S., gives correspondents great credit for providing protection for the dissidents—and Americans interested in civil liberties made regular calls to Sakharov until all international calls were blocked.

Artists like the sculptor E. I. Neizvestny, who wish to express themselves rather than official reality, are a problem to the regime. In the post-Stalin "thaw" Khrushchev invited Neizvestny and other prominent intellectuals to meet with the Central Committee, where, Khrushchev admits in his memoirs, he rudely criticized him. The former Chairman apologized for his pungent art criticism, and after his death his family commissioned the sculptor to do a mammoth head of Khrushchev for his grave. But Neizvestny's monumental, religious sculpture continued to offend those in power, and the KGB finally hounded him out of the country, forcing him to emigrate after sending some agents to break up some of his work with hammers.

Other targets of repression are minority nationalities such as the Crimean Tatars and the Lithuanians (who, in addition to being nationalists, practice a brand of Catholicism the party considers especially subversive). According to Edward Kline, the Soviets did try to relocate some of the Tatars in their historic homelands, but relocation is difficult when lands are already occupied by others, and respect for local language and culture, which is another important matter of contention in the Soviet Union, presents problems since Russian is the language of science, education, and government and the key to personal advancement to the highest reaches of the society.

The biggest increase in repression since Helsinki has been in Eastern Europe, particularly Poland, Czechoslovakia, and East Germany, where both the activism of dissidents and government repression have escalated. In some instances the methods employed by these governments are more repressive than in the U.S.S.R. The increase of social unrest and the government moves to control it are directly related to the worsening economic picture, particularly the rise of inflation. One of the paradoxes of détente is that economic interdependence, which does have liberalizing effects on formerly "closed societies," may also lead to repression. The more a formerly autarchic society is drawn into the world economy the more it suffers from the effects of economic downturns and inflation, which in turn lead to social unrest and heavy-handed policies to combat it.

Helsinki has increased expectations of liberalization and given a certain legitimacy to demands for freedom. But procedural freedoms, particularly freedom of association and expression, pose serious problems for the regime exactly for the same reasons they are valued in democratic theory. They are levers of change in the hands of citizens, and the sort of change they induce is not always easily controlled from the top. Khrushchev expressed the fear of the Soviet bureaucrat in confronting the forces of change when he described his own attitude toward the post-Stalin "thaw":

> We were scared—really scared. We were afraid the thaw might unleash a flood, which we wouldn't be able to control and which could drown us. How could it drown us? It could have overflowed the banks of the Soviet riverbed and formed a tidal wave which would have washed away all the barriers and retaining walls of our society.

The Helsinki agreements also provide for a greater two-way flow of information. But the pace is slow, and fear of ideological contamination remains high. Forty copies of *Le Monde* and sixty copies of the Paris *International Herald Tribune* are sent each day to the U.S.S.R. for occasional display in tourist hotels. They are not available for ordinary Soviet citizens. One of the perquisites of a research position in the Institute for the Study of the United States and Canada is access to American newspapers and magazines. Soviet researchers are avid readers of *U.S. News & World Report* and *Newsweek*. (But even here Glavlit, the censorship bureaucracy, intervenes. A researcher told me that political cartoons are regularly excised from copies of American magazines sent to the institute.)

The Soviets continue to jam Radio Liberty, which is staffed by emigrés and is strongly anti-Soviet in tone, but they do not jam Voice of America, the official propaganda arm of the U.S. Government. The Soviets have eased the travel restrictions for journalists working in the Soviet Union, and détente has made reporting from the Soviet Union a more pleasant and fruitful experience. The United States is pressing for a greater flow of books from the West into the Soviet Union. The Association of American Publishers has proposed that an American bookstore be opened in Moscow, but the Soviets appear unenthusiastic. The first joint Soviet-American feature film, *Bluebird,* has been made, and a second coproduction, *Sea Pup,* is scheduled for 1977. Cultural exchanges of pianists, ballets, and museum exhibits have increased. There is much more contact among university officials and increased interest in academic exchanges.

Whether the U.S.-Soviet relationship will grow warmer or colder depends to a great degree on domestic forces within the two societies. In the United States, despite the fact that the two major parties have not essentially disagreed on what it is or how to fight it, the cold war has played a crucial symbolic role in every election since the war. "Let's face it," a Republican adviser remarked in early 1952, "the only excuse for Ike's candidacy is that he's the man best qualified to deal with Stalin." Foreign policy issues are not debated in campaigns. They are used to create public moods. Campaign promises on foreign policy issues—from Franklin Roosevelt's 1940 pledge "Your boys are not going to be sent into foreign wars" to Nixon's secret plan to end the Indochina war with honor—are notoriously unreliable and unredeemable. The public mood is volatile and easily molded by those who speak with the authority of the White House or the Pentagon. It springs from a deep yearning for peace on one hand and a deep sense of insecurity on the other.

The causes of insecurity are complex, but as the Second World War ended, the symbol of national insecurity in America became Russia and world communism. The insecurity had less to do with the reality of Russian power—much of the Soviet Union was still in ashes—than with the bureaucratic revolution in the United States and the staggering social and political upheavals that accompanied World War II. Old values were crumbling. Small-town America was disappearing from whole regions of the country. For many Americans the life of the farm, the close family, and the rooted community were over. Thanks to the melting pot of military service, the racial migrations of the war years, and the revolution in communications and transportation, the United States for the first time in its history was a continental society. The atom bomb brought a credible picture of national catastrophe to Americans for the first time in almost a hundred years and contributed to a general anxiety. But more pervasive than the prospect of a common death under a mushroom cloud was the fear of what the new common life would be.

With the breakdown of old associations—family, church, community, and small business—Americans began to identify more and more with the state in Washington to give purpose and meaning to individual lives. To be sure, the old Jeffersonian ideology persisted. As necessary as they were in supplying Social Security checks, farm supports, and government contracts, bureaucrats in Washington were still felt to be meddlers when it came to domestic affairs. But in the world of national security, bureaucrats became statesmen, protectors of the land, and spokesmen for the nation. They expressed what it meant to be an American at a time when American identity was becoming more and more of a confusing notion. No longer a Jeffersonian network of "ward republics" where face-to-face politics could flourish or a racially homogeneous national state, America was reaching for a new identity. Mid-century America no longer promised the perfectibility of man. It was no longer the exclusive or even the preferred political model for colonial peoples. What characterized America was now its power, and the citizen's sense of belonging was somehow related to the vicarious exercise of national power. More and more an American came to mean someone who identified with the struggle against America's enemies. Americanism became defined in terms of un-Americanism.

By the end of World War II the revelations of the Soviet atomic spy rings and Stalin's brutality in Eastern Europe—the dimensions of his twenty-year war on his own people were not yet widely understood—had fanned latent anticommunist sentiments in the United States. Despite wartime propaganda about the brave Soviet ally, suspicion of Russia remained high. Stalin's empire was a symbol of atheism, totalitarianism, and subversion. The anticommunism of the Palmer raids, the Dies Un-American Activities Committee, and the 1930s ordinance of the Cambridge city council forbidding the public library to keep books with the words "Lenin" or "Leningrad" in them was now reinforced by what came to be known as McCarthyism.

A powerful coalition of forces emerging at the end of the war turned the latent anticommunism of the American people into the ideology of the cold war. One important element was the labor movement. In the first five years after the war the issue of the Soviet Union and what it was up to became enmeshed in political struggles between communists and non-communists for power over such critical American unions as the United Auto Workers. Anticommunism was a political weapon in these struggles. It was reinforced by passionate ideologues such as Jay Lovestone, former secretary-general of the American Communist party, who for thirty years guarded the ideological purity of the AFL by making sure that the dominant labor organization was faithful in its support for high military budgets, foreign wars, and paramilitary interventions and in its opposition to détente. Lovestone's retirement has made little difference. George Meany broke with Senator Henry Jackson, a hard-liner on détente, because he was the author of a compromise trade bill and Meany wanted no trade bill at all. Détente, he says, is "appeasement to dictators." "If the Western nations would grant the Soviet government the economic concessions it seeks," the AFL-CIO Executive Council declared shortly before the second Nixon-Brezhnev summit, "they would not be serving the interests of the Russian people, but rather the aims and designs of their oppressors and exploiters."

When Nikita Khrushchev visited the United States in 1959 he was toasted by bankers, but his talk with Walter Reuther, head of the United Auto Workers, "left an unpleasant taste in my mouth," he later wrote. American labor leaders see the men in the Kremlin as destroyers of unionism—trade unions are instruments of the state in the U.S.S.R.— and Russian politicians see American trade unionists as opportunists and traitors to their class. It is hard to find a labor leader who will press vigorously for détente. The American Committee on U.S.-Soviet Relations, a citizens' group for supporting détente which includes John Kenneth Galbraith, Theodore M. Hesburgh, president of Notre Dame, Jerome Wiesner, president of M.I.T., and such businessmen as Donald Kendall of

Pepsico and Robert Schmidt of Control Data, has little labor representa-
tion. The Committee on the Present Danger, on the other hand, a citizens'
committee to alert the country of the dangers of détente and the Soviet
military buildup, has Lane Kirkland, secretary-treasurer of the AFL-CIO
and Meany's likely successor, as president. Kirkland played a vigorous
role after Carter's election in pressing for the appointment of hard-line
officials in the Department of Defense and in blocking several candidates
suspected of being too soft on the Soviet threat.

Except for a few left-wing labor leaders, most of whom were purged
in the early postwar period, labor leaders have been skeptical of détente
initiatives. (Leaders of multinational firms, on the other hand, in the early
postwar period as in more recent times, have been transfixed by the prospect of an arrangement with the Kremlin to turn the Eurasian land mass
into a vast market for American goods and technology.) Two important
influences have made labor leaders especially susceptible to the fierce
ideology of recanted communists. One has been the Catholic Church.
Francis Cardinal Spellman was a public defender of Senator Joseph Mc-
Carthy at the height of his rampage, and Father Edmund Walsh of the
Georgetown School of Foreign Service was his mentor. The Kennedy
détente, symbolized by the American University speech calling for an end
to the cold war, would probably not have happened had it not come on the
heels of Pope John XXIII's encyclical *Pacem in Terris,* which represented
a substantial easing of the Church's traditional position on dealing with
communism. The other influence was the ethnic minorities from Eastern
Europe, who are heavily represented in some major unions. Each year a
powerful lobby succeeds in persuading the Congress to pass a resolution
proclaiming Captive Nations Week. In recent years their influence on
foreign policy has waned. All the Czech voters in Chicago could not move
the Johnson administration to more than a mild protest when the Soviets
invaded Czechoslovakia in 1968. But in 1946, Republican successes with
East European ethnic minorities were crucial in wresting control of the
Congress from the Democrats, and even more crucial in educating the Truman administration to the political value of hard-line anticommunism.

In recent years the ethnic minority with the greatest influence on the
politics of détente has been the Jews. The National Conference on Soviet
Jewry organized a grass roots campaign in support of the Jackson Amendment, which was an attempt to make economic concessions to the Soviet
Union conditional upon Soviet agreement to let 60,000 Jews a year leave
Russia. In response Nixon invited fifteen prominent Jewish leaders, including Jacob Stein, chairman of the Conference of Presidents of Major

American Jewish Organizations, to the White House to explain why more Jews would probably leave the Soviet Union if there were no Jackson Amendment. A complicated three-way negotiation ensued between Senator Jackson, the secretary of state, and the Soviets, who, it turned out, were willing to give informal undertakings to the U.S. Congress that 45,000 Jews could leave, but would make no public commitment. Senator Jackson's campaign was motivated in part by his interest in getting the support of Jewish leaders in his race for the presidency in 1976, and in part by moral concern reinforced by strong pressure from members of his staff, some of whom were Jewish.

The negotiation degenerated into a dispute acrimonious on all sides, Jackson accusing Kissinger of misleading him, Kissinger privately accusing Jackson of political grandstanding at the expense of the Soviet Jews, and the Soviets accusing the Americans of introducing the issue after the trade agreement had been negotiated and inflating it in response to Brezhnev's unilateral concessions. The explicit bargain over Soviet Jews failed. It is now evident that crude forms of linkage such as the Jackson Amendment do not work. In reaction to the direct effort to set internal Soviet policy the Soviets refused to put the trade agreement into effect and drastically curtailed the flow of Jewish emigration. Just as they had unilaterally liberalized their emigration policy to set the stage for economic agreements they wanted—in part in reaction to the U.S. debate on the Jackson Amendment—so they unilaterally reversed the policy when the United States attempted to make emigration an explicit condition of doing business.

But the behind-the-scenes negotiation continues and clearly has an impact on Jewish emigration from the Soviet Union. Soviet officials say privately that if the public pressure is removed, the Jewish community in the United States "will be pleased at what will happen," but demands for commitments to explicit levels of emigration will continue to be treated as an affront to Soviet sovereignty. "What would you think if we tried to force you to change your emigration policy?" they ask.

It is not surprising that official harassment of Soviet Jews should outrage Jews in America. What is extraordinary, as Joseph Albright notes in his account in *The New York Times* of "the deal to buy Jews from Russia," is that the moral position of an ethnic minority representing 3 percent of the American population could cause a country such as the Soviet Union to moderate its internal police policies. Even more significant for détente is that a traditionally liberal and antimilitarist minority has been drawn by two issues—Soviet military aid to the Arabs and the plight of the Soviet

Jews—to take a hard line on U.S.-Soviet relations and a skeptical view of cutting the military budget.

McCarthyism, the political use of anticommunism by a generation of American politicians, has left a permanent stamp on American politics. The fear of a right-wing reaction to "soft" policies has kept American Presidents on tougher courses *vis-à-vis* the Russians and communism than they might otherwise have taken. In his memoirs Roger Hilsman, who was in charge of intelligence in the State Department at the time, concludes that the country may not have been in mortal danger as a result of Khrushchev's placing some missiles in Cuba, "but the Administration certainly was." It was two weeks before the congressional elections, and a Republican senator, Kenneth Keating, was charging Kennedy with reckless disregard of national security. "If you hadn't acted, you would have been impeached," Robert Kennedy told his brother. The problem was not the military balance, which the secretary of defense had said was unchanged, but political vulnerability. Ten years later Henry Kissinger was privately saying much the same sort of thing. American withdrawal from Vietnam, he would tell his former colleagues from Harvard, would elicit a powerful right-wing backlash in the United States. It was fear of the right, not the left, that kept Lyndon Johnson on the same disastrous course in Indochina.

The second permanent effect on the demagogic uses of anticommunism was the collapse of the foreign policy debate. Politicians who felt uneasy about the militarization of American foreign policy, the immensity of the military budget, or making victory in the cold war America's national goal were afraid to expose themselves to the charge of being "Comsymps," in the Orwellian vernacular of the John Birch Society. The American Security Council, the John Birch Society, and other well-funded right-wing organizations held seminars, briefings, and forums throughout the country and inundated Congress with the rhetoric of Holy War. Until the Vietnam War there was nothing comparable on the other side, and then only in the years of crisis. A curious characteristic of the contemporary period is that the wave of progressive and reformist movements that emerged in the 1960s—the consumer movement, women's movement, minority-rights movements, environmental protection movement, and others—has been almost completely silent on the issues of war and peace. The new generation of political activists has had an instinctive aversion to enmeshing their special issues with the traditional cold-war issues on which so many of the liberals of the last generation lost their influence and their reputations.

Political support for détente is directly related to the military budget, which is the principal planning instrument for stabilizing the American economy. Under our system it is the only legitimate way the federal government can inject $50–$60 billion a year into the economy. (To spend it on houses or hospitals or health care would be socialism.) How and where these huge amounts of money are injected frequently determines which communities will flourish and which will die. Much has been made of the fact that the United States is spending a smaller percentage of its gross national product on defense than in the past, but other statistics are more politically relevant. One is the number of jobs that depend, directly or indirectly, on the military budget; according to the Arms Control and Disarmament Agency and Bureau of Labor Statistics, that figure may be as high as 14 million. The addiction of the American economy to ever increasing military spending is a reality that politicians ignore only at their peril. Their choices are to remove the addiction, a monumental task of reform involving the complete restructuring of the American economy (beating swords into plowshares is a good deal easier than changing missiles into subway systems), or to defend the escalating military budget by pointing to an escalating external threat. The greatest stumbling block to a domestic politics based on arms limitation and détente is the need for an enemy. It is not only the producers of military hardware in California and St. Louis who have such a need but the military bureaucrats in Washington—tens of thousands of dedicated, energetic people who have been well rewarded for worrying about the Soviet threat and have every incentive to dramatize it.

The domestic political forces inside the Soviet Union that affect détente are more difficult to discern. Clearly, the present policy of moderating the competition with the United States is Brezhnev's policy, a set of views and strategies to which his personal prestige has been committed. Equally clearly, the policy did not emerge without a struggle. On the day before Nixon arrived in Moscow in 1972 Brezhnev fired the anti-détente hardliner P. Y. Shelest from his seat on the Politburo, forcing him into the obscurity reserved for Soviet officials who miscalculate the balance of power in the Kremlin. Other indications of a struggle were a series of interviews with Soviet journalists and diplomats in the fall of 1970 and 1971 which criticized the German treaty which Brezhnev had just signed. Boris Rabbot, who was present at numerous discussions of détente involving various circles of the intelligentsia which, he says, reflect the different moods within the Politburo members themselves, confirms what one might expect: there were substantial disagreements within the Central Committee as to the value and practicality of the Brezhnev policy.

Thus, despite the extraordinary lengths to which the Soviets go to project "monolithic unity," it is evident that there are hard-liners and soft-liners on many issues surrounding détente. It is less clear how such factions relate to the principal institutions of Soviet life. Henry Kissinger has publicly suggested that their military are the hard-liners. "Both sides," he said in June 1974, "have to convince their military establishments of the benefits of restraint, and that does not come easily to either side." On one level that is true. On technical questions of arms control—how many missiles are equivalent to a submarine, how important is the "throw-weight" of a missile, in short, how much is enough for security—generals on both sides have a veto. Neither the President nor the Chairman will conclude an arms agreement to which his military establishment is strongly opposed. As we shall see, American generals have their own view of what Soviet generals *ought* to think is enough missiles and bombs to defend the Soviet Union. Soviet generals have a different view from their American counterparts as to what the Pentagon needs for defense, and that is why it is difficult to arrive at arms-control agreements that actually cut into military power. But this is not to say that the military establishment in the Soviet Union is any more an independent source of political power in the Soviet Union than is our military establishment in the United States. Indeed there is a good deal of evidence that it is less of one.

Russia has a history of lumbering military establishments under effective civilian control. There are no Latin American military conspiracies in Russian history, no Napoleon, not even the equivalent of a Washington or an Eisenhower at the head of the state. When Khrushchev decided to get rid of the popular Marshal G. A. Zhukhov, after the general had helped him oust Molotov and his friends in the "anti-party group" from the Politburo, he hinted darkly of the dangers of "Bonapartism," knowing the warning would strike a responsive chord among the Russian people.

The military is an interest group with which the Soviet leadership must negotiate on matters within their concern. It has great and growing power. It is subject to the same bureaucratic rhythms that produce the inexorable expansion of the Pentagon budget. But it continues under the firm control of the party. Although Soviet military journals carried skeptical articles about arms control in the early years when SALT I was under discussion, and arms-control specialists at the Institute for the Study of the U.S.A. and Canada tell American colleagues that Soviet generals are interchangeable with Pentagon generals, it is misleading to assume as William Odom, a U.S. Army student of the Soviet military, puts it "that military officers have become the key decision-makers—or decision-blockers—in Soviet foreign policy."

Just as the militarization of the U.S. economy and foreign policy was the decision of lawyers and bankers on loan to the national security establishment—Stimson, Forrestal, Acheson, Dulles, Nitze, McCloy—not generals, so also the militarization of the Soviet economy is the result of party pressure, not a military cabal. Over drinks Soviet diplomats sometimes speak to their American counterparts of the Soviet version of the military-industrial complex, the joint operations of military officers and the civilian managers of the armaments industry. But as Michel Tatu, the French Kremlinologist, points out, "in the U.S.S.R. the armaments industry does not seem to constitute a power really distinct from its principal customers, the military." When one of their number, such as Dmitri Ustinov, the current minister of defense, joins the Politburo his job is to present the viewpoint of the military bureaucracies at the highest levels. (Incidentally, it is worth noting that in 1967 the uniformed military were able to block the appointment of Ustinov, a civilian specialist in military production, in favor of Marshal Grechko, but could not do it again six years later.)

The power of military bureaucrats within the Soviet Union is growing because military bureaucracies have grown. The party has an elaborate structure to maintain control over the military. Ninety percent of the officers are Communists. Political officers (*politruki*) are spread throughout the forces with the task of conveying the line of the top military leadership and of preventing dissidence. But, Tatu argues, the party has had to share power with the military, the diplomatic service, and the police. As the power of ideology wanes, the classical institutions that undergird traditional great powers assume larger importance.

The role of the Soviet military is not only to project power abroad but to perform crucial tasks at home. The army in the Soviet Union carries out a variety of duties in the domestic economy which would be unthinkable in the United States. (It runs the television network in central Asia for example.) In a command economy the army may be the only ready source of manpower to carry out an urgent task. Thus some years ago a building that was to be a centerpiece of an international exposition burned a few days before the opening. Almost overnight hundreds of soldiers arrived on the scene and the building was restored in time for the ceremony. Without special intervention such a construction project would take months. The special role of the military is a measure of its importance in

Soviet life but it also is a factor to be considered in assessing the Soviet military budget. A good part of what the Soviet Union spends on its military does not go to the projection of military power but for the operation of the domestic economy.

A centrally planned command economy must rely on military-type organization. Since both economic and moral incentives play a relatively weak role, the economy depends upon a hierarchy for telling people what to do, which is exactly what an army is. Some Soviet émigrés argue that the Soviet Union can get along with a substantially smaller army only if it changes the organization of the internal economy.

The military is professionally skeptical about each arms-control proposal emanating from the West, but it does not appear to be anti-détente. Indeed, it could be argued, the Brezhnev policy serves their interest. It is building an environment for the rationalization and modernization of the forces at the same time it is reducing the risks that they will be used. Generals everywhere are as cautious about committing forces to battle as they are extravagant in collecting them. Soviet generals, who remember the high costs of martial glory in the civil war and in World War II, are more cautious than most. Soviet military doctrine and the Soviet weapons building program, as President Nixon once explained in a televised press conference, are heavily defense-oriented. Outside of the Soviet sphere established in World War II, the Soviets have not committed their forces in battle (with the exception of a hundred-odd pilots and technicians who were advisers to combat units in Korea and Egypt). Military power is a symbol of political and economic power. "Most probably Brezhnev and the marshals share the same view of the role of armed force," says Michel Tatu, "that is, that it should influence the course of world affairs by its presence alone and from that presence derive political advantage." It is also a visible measure of economic strength, a contemporary potlatch which separates those powers at the pinnacle who can maintain extravagant displays of military might from those who can't.

CHAPTER 4

The Image of the Enemy

The popular image of the Soviet Union in the United States has shifted, sometimes abruptly, over the last sixty years. International gangsters in the twenties, brave allies against fascism in the early forties, would-be world conquerors in the late forties, masters of subversion in the sixties, the managers in the Kremlin acquired a new reputation in the Kissinger era as amiable bureaucrats with a vested interest in the status quo who still bear watching. Public opinion polls swung dramatically as one image after another was projected. In late 1976, however, after a period in which George Kennan described U.S. relations with the Soviet Union as "fully as cordial as those with most of the European NATO members," the specter of Soviet militarism was revived. A new Committee on the Present Danger, made up mostly of prominent former national security managers, was formed to reawaken the country to the dangers of the Soviet military buildup, which Ronald Reagan made so important a part of his primary campaign. A 1976 poll by Potomac Associates, which in two previous years had shown a declining concern with the Soviet Union as a military threat, began to show rising public apprehension about Soviet military strength and greater willingness to support a larger U.S. defense budget.

The public image is a reflection of the official view of the Soviet Union, and that view is a composite of the impressions of a handful of individuals whose job it is to decide what the Soviets are up to and what the United States should do about it. With few exceptions—George Kennan and Charles Bohlen, for example—these individuals have not been professional Russian experts or Sovietologists. They have for the most part been bankers and lawyers for bankers, who selectively listen to "experts" but construct their image of the enemy from their own experience. There has been a remarkable consensus among that group that has evolved over thirty years, a legacy of such men as Dean Acheson, George Kennan, Averell Harriman, James Forrestal, Clark Clifford, who developed the early analysis of the cold war in the Truman administration.

Clark Clifford is one of the handful of influential advisers at the start of the cold war who looks at the Soviet Union through the same prism that served him thirty years ago but he sees a new image. He is an ardent supporter of improved relations with the U.S.S.R. and believes dramatic improvement is possible. A shrewd and well-paid lawyer, an architect of Truman's successful campaign in 1948, a hard-liner who became an opponent of the Vietnam War, Clifford was never a Russian expert. But he played a key role in the summer of 1946, as counsel to President Truman, in assembling the views of those who did claim to be Russian experts into a top-secret report that became the first official image of the enemy. It is an alarmist document, so frightening, Clifford recalls, that President Truman ordered him to destroy all but one copy and lock that one up in the President's own safe. "It could blow the lid off the world," Truman told him.

The picture of the Kremlin that emerges from the report is of "a small group of able men" blessed with "a remarkable ability for long-range forethought" who believe that "peaceful coexistence of communist and capitalist nations is impossible." Their "haunting sense of insecurity inherited from the past" and their belief that capitalism must be destroyed means that "we must assume that the USSR might fight at any time for the twofold purpose of expanding the territory under communist control and weakening its capitalist opponents." Clifford marshals the evidence in the manner of a brief, compiling a record of broken agreements in Germany and Eastern Europe, and Soviet espionage in the United States. The conclusion is stark. The United States "must be prepared to wage atomic and biological warfare if necessary," because "the language of military power is the only language which disciples of power politics understand."

Reflecting on the document thirty years later, Clifford thinks the concern was justified but the analysis was out of focus. When the men of the Truman administration who were trying to make sense of the new world emerging from the smoke of war looked into Stalin's face they saw Hitler. They had underestimated one dictator by ignoring *Mein Kampf*. To avoid making the same mistake, they dabbled in Marx and Lenin. Stalin, they believed, was dedicated to the Leninist thesis that sooner or later there would be a war with the capitalist world. Communist orthodoxy maintained that the capitalists would start the war in a desperate effort to save their system, but that was not particularly reassuring to the American elite. If the Soviets were paranoid, they might indeed, out of genuine but misguided defensive fears, trigger the "series of frightful clashes" that Lenin warned were "inevitable."

Clifford is a passionate defender of Truman and his advisers. He is no revisionist and thinks that the tough line taken in 1946 was justified. But he concedes that the Hitler analogy distorted the official image of the enemy at the highest levels of the administration. Stalin's fears of the West, which he believes were irrational, were nevertheless real, and they were seriously underestimated in Washington. The American strategy of talking to the Soviets "in the language of military power" led not to a softening of Soviet policy but to a hardening and to an arms race.

Clifford thinks three things have happened over thirty years to change the outlook of Soviet leaders from what it was when he prepared the memorandum for President Truman. First, since Khrushchev's time the Kremlin has publicly and officially proclaimed that war is not inevitable in the nuclear age and that indeed it is not a viable policy even for a dying capitalist system. That doctrinal revision, it should be noted, is far more than shallow propaganda, because the political costs for the Soviets of enunciating it have been enormous. Khrushchev's position on the horrors of nuclear war was at the heart of the dispute with Mao, who accused the Soviet leader of tampering with Marxist theory to "blackmail" the rest of the world into accepting U.S.-Soviet hegemony.

Second, the "closed society" that appeared so threatening in 1946 has been partially penetrated. The tight ideological control of the Kremlin has been broken somewhat by the increased flow of information. Soviet citizens can listen to the foreign radio. There is much more contact with foreigners. Soviet citizens travel abroad in greater numbers. It is still a tightly controlled system, but it is much harder to keep Soviet citizens in the dark about what is going on. The men who rule Russia are not as dangerous as in Stalin's day, so the theory goes, because they cannot manipulate public opinion to the same extent.

Third, the increased emphasis on consumer goods Clifford finds reassuring. "In 1974 we had 11 million cars in this country. The Soviets had 220,000. They had only one TV for every six families. There is a national longing for consumer goods, and this crowd knows that they must satisfy that longing or eventually the people will get a new crowd." Clifford is convinced that the Soviets do not have the resources to continue the arms race at the present level and that they have powerful domestic political incentives to cut the arms budget. All this makes the picture look very different from that in Stalin's day.

W. Averell Harriman holds the record for longevity and continuous influence among the Russian experts at the top of the U.S. Government. No individual played a larger role in defining the official image of the adversary. "In looking back over my experiences with the Soviet Union," he writes, "I find my basic judgments remain little altered, although conditions have changed radically." Like Clifford, he defends the basic decisions of the cold war but also heartily approves of détente, since, he says, the word means nothing more than relaxation of tensions, and one can hardly be against that. The term, however, has been oversold, he claims, to mean much more than can be achieved. The Soviets are genuinely interested in avoiding nuclear war, but they have not accepted the status quo everywhere in the world, as some Americans naïvely believe, and no understandings to that effect have been made.

Harriman, who used to have a signed photograph of himself and Stalin behind his desk at the State Department when he was undersecretary of state in the Johnson era, has been dealing with the Russians for fifty years. In 1924 he arranged a manganese concession in the Caucasus, hired a private railroad car to visit it, and got his money out with a modest profit. "The Soviet government, as in other financial transactions, lived up to its commitments," but the Bolshevik Revolution, he decided, was a "reactionary development," because "the individual must be the servant of the state." During the war years he was Roosevelt's special envoy to Stalin and, later, ambassador to the Soviet Union. More than anyone else Harriman promoted the "Stalin is the Hitler of today" analogy. In late April 1945 Harriman told Navy Secretary Forrestal, "We might well have to face an ideological warfare just as vigorous and dangerous as fascism or Nazism." Within a year he was telling the Business Advisory Council, a group of the most prominent industrialists and bankers in the country, that we should be tough with the Russians even at the risk of war. "Harriman thinks we are in the same position relative to Russia in 1946 as we were relative to Germany in 1933," Henry Wallace wrote in his diary on reading the speech.

Harriman saw Stalin as a shrewd and cautious political leader—so cautious in fact that, despite dozens of intelligence reports warning of

Hitler's plans, he postponed mobilization in June 1941 until three hours before the German attack so as not to provoke his erstwhile ally. But he would not hesitate to expand Soviet power if the cost were acceptable. Harriman was afraid, he recalls in his memoirs, that "Stalin's insistence upon a belt of weak, easily dominated neighboring states might not be limited to Eastern Europe." The danger was that Stalin "would probably attempt to penetrate the next layer of adjacent countries. He saw no virtue in waiting; the issue was best fought out as far to the east as possible." He defends the Yalta agreements on "free elections" in Eastern Europe because he thinks that "Stalin meant to keep his word, at least within his own interpretation." It is a mistake, he says, to assume that Stalin had a "fixed plan" to impose communist governments in Eastern Europe. "He doubtless expected that the Red Army would be welcomed everywhere as a liberating force. I am inclined to believe that the Communist leaders in these countries greatly overestimated their popularity and reported in that vein to Moscow. In short, Stalin at first mistakenly believed that there was little risk in promising free elections because the Communists were popular enough to win."

Harriman had a crucial role in setting the tone of U.S. policy toward the Soviet Union in the days immediately after Roosevelt's death. In his last weeks F.D.R. had begun to express concern about Stalin. "Averell is right. We can't do business with Stalin. He has broken every one of the promises he made at Yalta," Anna Rosenberg recalls him saying at lunch on March 23. To Anne O'Hare McCormick of *The New York Times,* who saw the President the day he left for the final trip to Warm Springs, Roosevelt said that either Stalin was not in control of the Soviet Government or he was not a man of his word.

When Truman came to the White House, Harriman kept pushing for a tough reappraisal of U.S. policy toward the Soviet Union by promoting a picture of the Soviet dictator, whom few others in the U.S. Government had met, as a man over whom the United States had considerable "leverage" if we would use it, but who would seek to control everything he could "by bluffing." The Soviet Union, he said, was "fantastically backward." The Soviets needed heavy machinery. They had no modern roads, no adequate railroad system, and 90 percent of Moscow's population lived in wretched conditions. In short, he was "not much worried about the Soviet Union's taking the offensive in the near future." The United States should take a tough line and use its economic power to make the Soviets behave.

Harriman continually stressed how difficult it was to do business with the Russians. His memoirs are filled with irritating incidents of prolonged and meaningless negotiations, minor harassments, suspicion, and personal unpleasantness. The style of Stalinist Russia in wartime was forbidding, and it made a deep impression upon those who would set U.S. policy toward the Soviet Union. Secretary of War Henry Stimson, who had doubts about the tough policy Harriman was recommending, thought he was overly influenced by his "past bad treatment" at the hands of the Russians. Curiously, Stalin himself was adept at charming Americans. Truman's election gaffe in 1948—"I like old Joe. He's a prisoner of the Politburo"—reflected official feelings in Washington during the war. Molotov and the generals were dour. Stalin made pleasantries, and when important concessions were to be made, he was the one who made them. Cordell Hull was so impressed with the Soviet dictator that he noted in his diary after leaving his presence: "I thought to myself that any American having Stalin's personality and approach might well reach high public office in my own country."

It was precisely to counteract the euphoria and naïveté of the wartime alliance that George Kennan developed his theory of the "sources of Soviet conduct" and advanced his "containment" thesis. Roosevelt's hopes for enlisting cooperation of the Soviet leaders in the postwar world were naïve, because "there can never be on Moscow's side any sincere assumption of a community of aims between the Soviet Union and powers which are regarded as capitalist." Since Soviet ideology had not been officially junked, Kennan wrote in 1946, the antagonism remains and from it flow "the secretiveness, the lack of frankness, the duplicity, and the basic unfriendliness of purpose." Stalin was not Hitler. He was "more sensitive to contrary force, more ready to yield on individual sectors of the diplomatic front when that force is felt to be too strong and thus more rational in the logic and rhetoric of power." There was no hope of banking goodwill by making concessions or trying to create a nonthreatening environment, because Soviet leaders would create the threat out of their own ideology anyway. Thus there was little to be gained by negotiation. Indeed, Kennan had recommended at the time that the United States should not bargain with Stalin at Yalta. The rational course was to divide Europe into two spheres of influence and accept no responsibility for what the Russians did in their sphere, because the United States was too weak to do anything about it. Kennan's prescription was "long-term, patient but firm and vigilant containment of Russian expansive tendencies," in the hope of

increasing "the strains under which Soviet policy must operate" and promoting tendencies "which must eventually find their outlet in either the
breakup or the gradual mellowing of Soviet power."

Kennan was the only influential adviser of the early postwar period who
was a professional student of the Soviet Union. His analysis was sufficiently subtle, and at crucial points ambiguous, to enable partisans of far
more simple policies to use it for their own purposes. Thus James Forrestal gave Kennan's cables wide circulation in the government to support
stronger military programs and an education campaign to alert the public
to the Soviet menace. Kennan later insisted that containment was not primarily a military idea, that the Soviets did not have a grand design for
conquest, that they were far weaker than Americans supposed and did
not intend to pursue their competition with the United States by means
of war. The best policy was "aimed at creating strength in the West rather
than destroying strength in Russia." The danger of war, Kennan argued
in 1950, was that the United States, through its military buildup and talk
of war, "might inadvertently convince them that it could not be avoided."

Kennan set the tone of official analysis of the "sources of Soviet conduct" by stressing the importance of ideology. The Soviet leaders were
implacably hostile because of their belief that they had an infallible guide
to understanding the forces of history, that these forces were moving inexorably their way, and that the ideological purity of the Soviet Union
must be preserved at all costs. Hence relations with the West must always
take the form of an "ideological struggle." Charles Bohlen, Kennan's
successor as ambassador to the Soviet Union and another professional
Russian expert, used to say that the Soviet Union was a cause, not a
country.

The one thing American politicians and Soviet politicians have usually
agreed upon since the beginning of the cold war is that they are engaged
in an "ideological struggle," but there has been a good deal of mystery
and confusion about the nature of that struggle. The term has been used
in several senses. When Kennan focused attention on ideology in his
influential cable from Moscow in 1946 and in the expanded version in
Foreign Affairs a year later, he was talking about the world view of the
Soviet leaders and why that world view made it difficult to do business
with them and why it was naïve to expect them to "cooperate" in building
a liberal, democratic, capitalist world. Convinced that the United States,
as the leading capitalist state, is out to destroy them, and that they can
find security only if capitalist power is broken, the Kremlin moves patiently

but inexorably "wherever it is permitted to move. . . . Its main concern is to make sure that it has filled every nook and cranny available to it in the basin of world power." The ideology, according to this interpretation, is expansionism, not communism. Stalin's interest was not world revolution but a world increasingly subject to Soviet domination. Communism was the fig leaf to disguise the nakedness of Soviet imperial expansion, an instrument for legitimizing conquest.

As depressing a prospect as this was, it was less pessimistic than the rival theory that several American politicians found congenial and that J. Edgar Hoover popularized in his speeches and a best-selling book. The ambitions of the men in the Kremlin transcended the borders of their mammoth state, which stretched across one-sixth of the earth's surface. They were a band of international conspirators, propelled by a religious faith that they were riding the wave of history. There was no way to deal with them except to destroy them. Kennan, at least, saw the possibility that the responsibility of running a huge state would require some accommodation to the real world, and that would mean moderating the paranoid world view of the Kremlin. It was a way of confronting Soviet leaders with the reality of America's superior power and forcing Soviet accommodation. But containment was a crude theory that implied, whether Kennan wished it or not, the steady threat of military force. Its assumption that encircling the Soviet Union with bases would make Soviet leaders more accommodating was optimistic. The American diagnosis of the Russian problem was paranoia, and the prescription was to project an ever greater military threat. Indeed, the prescription was written before the diagnosis was made. "The army is insisting on complete encirclement of Russia with air bases in Iceland, Greenland, the Aleutians, and Okinawa," the columnist Joseph Alsop tells Henry Wallace at a dinner party in January 1946. Wallace recalls that Alsop, who was to make his career in his influential column articulating the alarmism of Pentagon weapons procurers, "says frankly that if he were Russia, seeing this going on, he would declare war on the United States at once."

A persistent idea in the American strategy for confronting the Soviet Union is that the ideological struggle must be resolved through internal change in the U.S.S.R. The popular notion of convergence implies far more fundamental change in the Soviet Union than in the United States. Franklin Roosevelt, Harriman recalls, "was in a sense a forerunner of the present-day convergence school. His New Deal revolution had expanded American ideas about the government's social responsibility; he confidently believed this trend would continue after his own time. In the Soviet Union, he saw the completely centralized state bureaucracy giving way to a degree of decentralization." The justification for using American power to change Soviet society was that if the Soviets became more like the Americans in their values, in the organization of their society, they would become less dangerous.

Why this was so was never clear. Most wars in history have been fought by tribes, nations, and empires that were rather similar in the values they pursued and in the way they organized their social structures. Indeed, they came into conflict precisely because they wanted the same things. Yet evidence that "the Russians are becoming more like us" has been reassuring to the U.S. national security elite because it symbolizes American power. When Soviet leaders define "building communism" as increasing the supply of nylons in the shops, easing the credit to enable a growing class of industrial and academic bureaucrats to buy cars, and making Italian-cut trousers instead of the baggy pants that used to be the uniform of every Russian male from Khrushchev down, they are accepting the American definition of the good life as the goal of the Russian Revolution. That is flattering and reassuring to American liberals. The fact that Brezhnev is an impeccable dresser and likes extravagant cars makes him easier to understand. Revolutionary ideology is a threat to established power because it challenges the purpose for which power is exercised. Revolutionary organization, even a radical vision of how to achieve traditional social values and goals, is much less of a challenge. One can have a polite debate about whether it is a good idea to nationalize industry, to have long-range economic planning, or to run a continental empire with a centralized bureaucracy. But an ideology that proclaims an entire social system to be the embodiment of wickedness precludes contact, much less accommodation. At the height of the cold war both sides used the rhetoric of disease to describe the system of the other. Communism was a virus, a social sickness, a disease of the body politic. Capitalism, bourgeois culture, was a source of contamination, cancer, rot.

Soviet specialists in the State Department for the most part believe that convergence is a simplistic notion. But they do think that the ideological world view of the Soviet leaders that Kennan described in 1946 has changed. Brezhnev thinks in traditional Soviet categories and can talk no language other than the one developed by Lenin and Stalin, but he does not look at the world through the same ideological prism as Soviet leaders did thirty years ago. In the interim the Soviet elite has probably changed more ideas about how the contemporary world works than has the U.S. national security establishment. The significance of the Chinese revolution, the meaning of decolonization in the Third World, the role of nuclear weapons, the "crisis of capitalism," the role of Communist parties in West Europe—these are some of the areas in which fundamental changes in Soviet perceptions have occurred. It is hard to find changes of comparable significance in official U.S. thinking.

One of the dividends of détente, a senior State Department analyst notes, is that we can figure out better what Soviet leaders are saying. Soviet ideology, in his view, is primarily dangerous because it impedes communication. Ideology is not as much an intellectual straitjacket for Soviet leaders as it was a generation ago. Indeed, they are remarkably adept at adapting ideology to practical political needs. The problem is that the American elite does not understand the language. Ideological rhetoric is threatening because it has two characteristics that make American lawyers, bankers, and generals particularly uncomfortable—vagueness and passion. In person Soviet leaders are grayer than their rhetoric—and somewhat more precise. The more contact we make at all levels of Soviet society, and particularly at the highest, one U.S. intelligence analyst suggests, the better tools we have to understand the code in which Soviet leaders talk to each other. In the détente era it is possible for the first time in years for U.S. diplomats to meet the top ideologues in the Soviet Union. Not long ago Mikhail Suslov, the chief ideologue, received the American ambassador in the inner sanctum of the Central Committee, where no U.S. diplomat had ever been before, ostensibly to accept some ammunition for the elegant shotgun Nixon had presented to Brezhnev. For U.S. analysts to have the report of such a conversation, even though it was, as one might expect, rather stiff, is like finding a truffle or a pearl.

One form of ideological struggle, then, is the struggle of two elites with radically different backgrounds and perceptions to understand each other. The problem of communication is complicated because each elite wishes to reveal itself and to remain mysterious at the same time. Each wants to avoid miscalculation. Neither wants to telegraph important moves. The fascination of the two elites with each other creates a set of bargaining chips that are probably more effective for playing the new phase of the global game than trading weapons systems. The United States is interested in preserving a relationship in which the U.S. ambassador can unpeel some of the layers in which Soviet society is wrapped to discover the sources of Soviet conduct and to fathom long-term intentions. The Soviets treasure

the chance, denied them in predétente days, to send swarms of Third Secretaries into congressional offices to collect transcripts of hearings, reports,
and gossip. It was always possible for the Soviets to collect more information about the United States than they could possibly digest, but under
détente it is possible to talk to strategically located people who can provide
a clue to what the U.S. elite is thinking. Such information is far more
valuable than that which spies risk their lives to obtain.

A second form of ideological struggle concerns the internal political
development of both societies. Sixty years ago Lenin and Woodrow Wilson
were convinced that socialism and capitalism could not survive in the same
world. Despite the practical necessity of coexistence, the official eschatology in both Washington and Moscow still embraces the fantasy of mass
conversion—the day, as Walter Lippmann once put it, when Soviet babies
are born singing "God Bless America," or, in Khrushchev's prophecy,
when John F. Kennedy's grandchildren will live under communism. From
the start of U.S.-Soviet relations, each side has tried to induce internal
political change in the other out of a belief that its own security and power
demanded it.

For the Soviet Union the instrument in prewar days was the U.S. Communist party. Its role was not to make a revolution—which even at the
depths of the Depression was a remote prospect—but to build sympathy
for the Soviet Union and to help mold a left-liberal coalition for reforms
that would restrain the power of business and build a labor movement. A
liberal America would be less anti-Soviet than a conservative America.
With the destruction of the American Communist party in the cold war
and the purge of pro-Soviet officials from the New Deal bureaucracies at
the onset of the cold war, Soviet hopes for a transformation of American
society waned. Today Soviet ideology has been revised to accept the notion
that the "crisis of capitalism" will be prolonged, that the system has
extraordinary adaptive powers, and that socialism in the United States is
more likely to come about as a result of external pressures—a change in
the global "correlation of forces"—which eventually will force internal
adjustments. More important, Soviet ideologues now take the view that
capitalism no longer has the power to undermine the Russian Revolution.

Soviet leaders have always professed a faith that one day there would
be a socialist United States. There is no evidence that they are in a hurry
to see it. Indeed, if the prospect ever became credible, it would cause
panic in the Kremlin. The entry of China, an embryonic great power, into
the socialist camp posed a far greater ideological challenge to Soviet lead-

ership than anything the United States has done. Unlike China, the United States could put a developed economy at the service of a socialist state and would have far more standing to criticize the Kremlin's rule than a capitalist America. It would be difficult for the Soviet Union to preserve what is left of the fiction that it is the leader of the "socialist camp."

If the Soviet elite has been quite content to wait a long time for a political conversion in the United States, the American elite has been less patient about changes in Russia. From the time of the Russian Revolution it has been an article of faith in the United States that stable and peaceful relations required some fundamental changes inside the Soviet Union. It had to act more like a state and less like a cause. It had to offer as a condition of recognition in 1933 some vague assurances on cessation of subversive activities and equally unenforceable promises concerning religious freedom. When Secretary of War Stimson in 1945 raised the question with President Truman about sharing the atomic bomb with the Soviet Union, believing that U.S.-Soviet relations would be embittered by the nuclear-weapons issue, Mr. Truman's initial reaction was to "question whether we could be safe in sharing the atomic bomb with Russia while she was still a police state and before she put into effect provisions assuring personal rights and liberty to individual citizens." He concluded that "any demand for an internal change in Russia" would be resented and that the "change in attitude toward the individual in Russia will come slowly and gradually." At about the same time, Harry Hopkins was articulating what soon became the ideology of the Free World: "The American people want not only freedom for themselves but they want freedom for other people as well."

From Franklin Roosevelt to Jimmy Carter, the idea that America's mission was to spread freedom has taken many forms. At the start of the cold war the conflict with the Soviet Union was painted as a struggle to preserve not only the right of private property but also the rights of the individual against the state. It was standard political rhetoric, indeed the essence of the American ideology, that the two were inseparable. The United States could not rest until the people of Eastern Europe and the Russians themselves were free. But more than rhetoric was involved. The explicit object of certain U.S. policies, such as the Baruch plan for international control of atomic energy and the provision for on-site inspection for various disarmament schemes, was to "open up the Soviet Union" and to lend outside support to the forces in Soviet society that would eventually liberalize it from within. The ideological orientation of U.S. policy toward the Soviet

Union reached its high point in the era of John Foster Dulles, who believed, as a West German diplomat said of him, that "Bolshevism was a product of the devil and that God would wear out the Bolsheviks in the long run." Dulles' strategy and ideology was to characterize the Soviet Union as the embodiment of a vicious ideology and to encircle and threaten it, justifying it all as a moral crusade. Only the most minimal business could be done with them until their odious system was changed.

Today it remains U.S. policy to open up the Soviet Union and to influence it in the direction of liberalization. Henry Kissinger argued that détente has increased the flow of information in and out of Russia, protected the dissidents inside the Soviet Union, made it possible for thousands to leave, and has made the evolution of Soviet society toward liberalism more likely. To what extent that is true we will consider later. But it is clear that internal change is not, as it was for Woodrow Wilson, John Foster Dulles, or John F. Kennedy, a priority objective of American policy. In the Kissinger era, liberalization was no longer viewed as a precondition for a substantial improvement in U.S.-Soviet relations, and, even with the increased emphasis on human rights of the Carter administration, this is still the U.S. policy.

Kissinger believed in the "necessity of choice," a term he used as a title of one of his books. It was naïve to think that you could have peace with great powers and try to remake their societies at the same time. Stability required concrete agreements with leaders in power, however ideologically or morally offensive one might find them. A strong believer in a world managed by leaders in control of their societies, Kissinger was convinced that statesmen could not "give political science lectures" to one another. In a world of strategic choices, peace came before justice, and if that required clinking glasses with people who oppressed their own people, so be it. Kissinger's nostalgic vision of a nineteenth-century balance-of-power system rested on the seventeenth-century principle of international law, *cujus est regio, illius est religio*—whoever controls the territory may impose his own religion. Thus détente marked a crucial change in American ideology, the recognition of the legitimacy of the Russian Revolution and the acceptance of the Soviet Union, though still perceived as a hostile power, into the family of nations.

Kissinger's brand of realism fitted the historical moment in which he was called to exercise power. By 1969 the moralistic rhetoric of the Dulles-Kennedy-Johnson era had become a casualty of the Vietnam War. The political task for the U.S. President was disengaging from Southeast

Asia with the least damage to American prestige, not advertising the United States as the "guardian at the gates" or "defender of world freedom." The euphoria of the Kennedy days, when the American responsibility was defined as nation-building in Southeast Asia and the spreading of liberal democracy through the Alliance for Progress in Latin America, was over. All over the world the United States was cooperating with military dictatorships that had seized power by force of arms, in some cases with the active support of the CIA and the U.S. military. When Truman's secretary of state, James Byrnes, in the immediate postwar days accused the Soviet Union of reneging on its pledge to hold "free elections" in Poland, no one, not even Molotov, was indelicate enough to note that in Byrnes's native state, South Carolina, the Jim Crow elections were not free. In Kissinger's time the contradictions between the rhetorical commitment to freedom and human rights and the official silence with respect to the widespread violations of human rights in anticommunist countries made it difficult to continue a credible ideological crusade behind what used to be called the Iron Curtain.

In recent years the clash of ideologies has had less to do with the organization of American and Soviet society than with the organization of political power on a world scale. The third form of ideological struggle, the one that has captivated and confused U.S. national security managers since the late 1950s, is what used to be called the fight for the hearts and minds of people. More precisely, the fight has been over the political and economic system of underdeveloped countries. To the extent that former colonial societies chose some form of Marxism as a way of looking at the world, closed off the society to private investment, looked to the Soviet Union for material aid or political support, the United States lost prestige and power. As more societies rejected the American model of development, the United States would become increasingly isolated. Khrushchev once described his idea of peaceful coexistence as a decadent marriage between a rich old woman and a young man. The old lady would grow weaker as more and more of the world was detached from her influence. The young man would have affairs in the Middle East, Africa, and Latin America. Eventually the old lady would stop caring.

Khrushchev's fantasy became the official nightmare in Washington. As the 1960s began, one War of National Liberation had turned Cuba, a traditional American dependency, into a feisty revolutionary state and another threatened to undermine the base of American power in Southeast Asia. American leaders accepted much of Soviet rhetoric. "Today's struggle does not lie here," President Kennedy told Paul Henri Spaak on a visit to Europe in the last year of his life, "but rather in Asia, Latin America, and Africa." The less developed lands, John J. McCloy wrote in 1960, "promise to be the principal battleground in which the future shape of society may finally be tested and determined." The focus of U.S. foreign policy became counterinsurgency. In 1951 Dean Rusk had announced that Mao's China was a "colonial Russian government." Guerrilla warfare was neither a spontaneous nor an indigenous phenomenon. The revolutionary virus that kept Indochina inflamed for thirty years was exported from Moscow and Peking. The enemy was "world communism," whose master planners in the Kremlin, as John Kennedy put it, were "armed with revolutionary doctrines of class warfare and modern methods of subversion and terror." This was a force, Kennedy declared, the United States had to oppose everywhere—"two great powers contending with each other for sway over the destiny of man."

The ideological struggle looks different in the late 1970s. In Kissinger's map of the world, unlike Kennedy's, nationalism is a real force. The end of the Vietnam War marked the triumph of an independent revolutionary movement and the collapse of American power in the area, but not the extension of Soviet power or Chinese power. American intelligence analysts are aware of the efforts of the newly reunified Vietnam to remain free of control by either communist power—a strategy that includes negotiating with American oil companies. They are also aware that the Soviet Union gave the Allende government in Chile little aid even when U.S. intelligence agencies were investing heavily in strikes, propaganda, and terrorism to subvert a regime in which one of the strongest and most pro-Soviet communist parties in the world participated. The instruments of Soviet power in the Middle East were not communist parties—indeed the Soviet Union gave billions in military aid to countries that have outlawed their local communist parties—but politicians who were in the end, as it turned out, more responsive to Kissinger's vision of the good society than Brezhnev's. Under Sadat the vestiges of Nasser's brand of socialism are disappearing from Egypt.

Kissinger understood that the secret of successful counterinsurgency struggle, or in his language, the effort to maintain stability in the Third World, was to play on the conflict of interest between the Soviet state and the revolutionary movements. The success of the strategy was dramatized when Brezhnev agreed to receive Nixon just as the President had ordered the mining of Haiphong. The price of keeping revolutionaries from coming to power was to accommodate those that had already made it. The Russian and the Chinese revolutions were to be recognized as part of a strategy to keep the Vietnamese revolution or the Argentinian revolution from happening. As we have seen, Nixon believed that the Soviet Union would help him end the Vietnam War. Indeed, his original interest in détente grew out of that hope. Helmut Sonnenfeldt believes that the Soviet Union went as far as it could in exerting pressure on the Vietnamese to settle with the Americans on something close to Nixon's terms, but he thinks that Kissinger overestimated the power the Kremlin had over Hanoi.

In the mid-1970s the term "world communism" is an anachronism with meaning only for those who believe the Sino-Soviet dispute to have been a trick. However, the unceasing polemics and occasional military skirmish between the two communist nations are convincing enough to persuade most of the U.S. elite that the dispute is real. (The welcome in Peking of such anti-Soviet hard-liners as Franz Joseph Strauss and James Schlesinger and the conversion of the Chinese into ardent supporters of NATO is difficult to dismiss as an elaborate hoax.) But the crisis of world communism goes well beyond the Sino-Soviet dispute. In 1957 Mao Tse-tung could proclaim at a conference in the Kremlin that the Soviet party was "at the head of the communist world movement." By June 1969 another conference of communist parties declared that "there is no leading center of the international Communist movement." There are now 121 communist parties in 92 countries, of which only 65 are pro-Soviet. Despite major efforts of the Kremlin to restore an appearance of unity to the world communist movement, these have been successfully resisted. When Moscow finally succeeded in holding another "unity" conference in 1976, it was a disaster for the Kremlin. Enrico Berlinguer, the head of the Italian Communist party, publicly condemned the violation of human rights in the Soviet Union. It was as if a cardinal had gone to Rome to denounce the Pope. Georges Marchais, the head of the French Communist party, long one of the most subservient in the communist world, declared that the "dictatorship of the proletariat" was an old-fashioned idea that had no place in modern French politics. The new generation of West European communists—the press immediately dubbed them "Eurocommunists"— were now running for office on a declaration of independence. It was more than a humiliation for the Kremlin; it was a challenge to the authority of Soviet rule.

The crisis of authority in the world communist movement is the continuation of a process that began almost as soon as the Bolsheviks had seized power. At the first Comintern Congress, in 1919, Trotsky proclaimed the revolutionary faith of the time. "Our task is to mobilize the forces of all genuinely revolutionary parties of the world proletariat and thereby hasten the victory of the communist revolution throughout the world." The ease of the October Revolution, a swift and relatively bloodless coup, seemed to confirm the euphoric vision of a wave of revolutions. Bolshevism was an internationalist faith. The Russian Revolution was the base for the transformation of the world. It was not an end in itself. Indeed, Joseph Stalin, who a few years later would grasp total control of the Soviet state with the help of the slogan "Socialism in one country" and make communism an instrument of Russian power, was expressing the orthodoxy of the time when he wrote to a German comrade in 1923, "The victory of the German proletariat will undoubtedly shift the center of the world revolution from Moscow to Berlin." Four years later the vocabulary had changed. "A revolutionary is one who is ready to protect, to defend the USSR without reservation, without qualification, openly and honestly . . . An internationalist is one who is ready to defend the USSR without reservation, without wavering, unconditionally; for the USSR is the base of the world revolutionary movement and this revolutionary movement cannot be defended and promoted unless the USSR is defended." The U.S.S.R. reserved the right to decide what was a "revolutionary situation" and what was not and what tactics revolutionaries should employ.

In the first years after the Bolshevik Revolution the Soviet Government tried infiltrating Russian "insurgents" into Estonia, and fought a brief war with Poland (which the Poles started) under the banner of "revolution from without," but these efforts failed. Only in territories that had been part of the czarist empire of a Russian protectorate, such as Outer Mongolia, did the Soviets succeed in establishing a communist government. This was not the export of revolution but the consolidation of empire by military power. Popular uprisings, revolutionary ideology, or indeed internal politics of any kind had little to do with it. Beyond the reach of the Red Army, the Soviets soon abandoned the idea of supporting revolution. Even before Stalin took power, the Soviet Government had transformed the Comintern, the international organization of communist parties that was supposed to plan the world revolution, into an instrument of Kremlin policy. A principal function was to cool revolutionary zeal where it would embarrass the Soviet Government in its relations with other states. The strategy for the defense of the Russian Revolution was not to make revolutions elsewhere but to seek respectability for the Soviet state. To this end local communists would be sacrificed unhesitatingly.

Indeed, it was a small sacrifice, for Stalin sensed early in his rule that an independent communist revolution was a threat to Soviet interests. Stalin's advice to the Chinese communists in the 1920s to make peace with Chiang Kai-shek and to abandon the notion of a peasant-based communist revolution was a reflection not only of Stalin's natural caution but of his fear that a nonsubservient communist China with a different revolutionary path and a different value system might turn into an enemy. His premonition was of course correct. Not only China, but Yugoslavia and Albania, the only two countries in Europe to establish a communist revolution without the aid of the Red Army, have been hostile to the Soviet Union. For a time even Soviet relations with Cuba, despite almost fifteen years of million-dollar-a-day subsidies, were severely strained. The postwar expansion of the "socialist camp" was set by the reach of the Red Army, and only in those countries in which Moscow imposed its brand of socialism has the Kremlin been able to maintain control.

In the Kissinger era American analysts have a different conception of the role of ideology from those of their predecessors in the Dulles or the Rusk era. They have come to realize that the power and the stability of the Soviet state is not necessarily enhanced when a movement calling itself communist takes over the government in another country. Indeed, it usually is the source of friction. There is no Soviet model for export. Non-Russian communists around the world are sharpening their criticism of Soviet society and making it clear that they are not interested in replicating it. Indeed, the disillusionment in the Third World about the Soviet system is matched only by disillusionment with the American system. Both superpowers appear increasingly irrelevant as sources of inspiration and examples for building new societies in the former colonial world, though financial aid or political support from one or the other remains crucial in some cases. On the seventh floor of the State Department, where the secretary and his top aides sit, the notion is generally accepted that the Soviet Union seeks control over politicians in Third World countries, using money, blackmail, and occasionally assassination, but the purposes for which power is sought are traditional, not revolutionary. The Kremlin is much less interested in how these societies will organize themselves than in reducing U.S. influence over them and encouraging them to support the Soviet line on specific international issues.

A few years ago such views were common enough among professional analysts, but they were filtered through the prism of American true believers, such as Dulles, who relished the notion of ideological struggle. Believing that free enterprise and freedom were inseparable and that the

American economy was indeed a model for bringing prosperity to the world, Dulles was convinced that the United States had a moral duty to press for the liberation of Soviet-dominated areas of Europe and to maintain a quarantine of the Soviet Union to keep Stalin's successors from achieving the international respectability they so obviously wanted. To treat the Soviet Union as another great power, even an ambitious and dangerous one, instead of the center of a monolithic movement, would, as Dulles' biographer Townsend Hoopes has put it, "rob the West of what Dulles regarded as its indisputable and indispensable moral edge." If the West maintained military, political, and moral pressure upon the Soviet system, it would eventually collapse of its own inner moral decay. Every step toward negotiation violated his basic strategy of isolating and condemning the Soviet Union as a moral outrage. Dulles compromised with his own ideology. He made some important agreements with the Soviets, notably the Austrian State Treaty, which brought about the withdrawal of Soviet troops from that country, but he never concealed his feelings that he was dealing with lepers. His greeting of Chou En-lai at the 1954 Geneva Conference, when he brushed elbows with him to avoid shaking hands, symbolized his whole career in dealing with communism.

Dulles was probably the purest ideologue in power on either side in the U.S.-Soviet confrontation. He believed that the unlimited expansion of American power, through military pacts, bases surrounding the Soviet Union, and a relentless anti-Soviet diplomacy, was justified by the evil of Soviet power and made possible by the inherent weakness of their morally corrupt system. It was a mirror image of the communist view of capitalism —also an evil system destined to fall of its own weight but deserving of a push now and again. It was fashionable to patronize Dulles in the Kennedy White House for his crudeness and his zeal, but his influence persisted. The amazing failure of the Eisenhower and Kennedy administrations to perceive the reality of the Sino-Soviet split long after it had become public knowledge and to react to Khrushchev's broad hints on at least two occasions for a U.S.-Soviet alliance against China can be explained only by the fact that the U.S. national security managers were transfixed by the idea of fighting an ideology rather than a nation. They were still wearing Dulles' glasses.

In the détente years, ideological fervor has declined on both sides. In the United States there are increasing doubts about the capacity of the peculiarly organized mixed economy that Americans continue to call "free enterprise" to solve the problems of advanced industrial civilization

—inflation, unemployment, decay of the cities, pollution, and crime. Some top business leaders are, as the recent survey by Leonard Silk and David Vogel shows, openly expressing doubts about the compatibility of American democracy and the American economic system. The depressing results of the Decade of Development, which show rising unemployment, worsening income distribution, and increasing misery in the Third World, have convinced many former true believers that the optimism of Dulles' day about making the world rich by spreading the American model was an illusion. Having exhausted the intellectual capital of the New Deal, the American economic system appears headed for an era of transition in which some structural changes will be tried. A system that advertises its own self-doubt with talk of "the long nightmare" of Watergate and "the agony of Vietnam" loses its zeal for proselytizing and its attraction as a model. There is an increasing sense among the national security elite of America's ideological isolation, the problem of maintaining liberal capitalist democracy in one country in a world that is clearly not heading in that direction.

The ideological friends of America, who dominated European politics in the first postwar generation—Alcide De Gasperi, Paul Henri Spaak, Robert Schumann, Konrad Adenauer—were all Christian Democrats, and they were enthralled by America—but they are gone. The America-oriented parties, such as the Christian Democrats in Germany, have grown weaker, or, as in Italy, have been seriously discredited because of corruption. The new friends of the United States on which the Kissinger structure of peace (inherited by Carter) depends are for the most part authoritarian regimes.

The absence of ideological fervor within the Soviet Union has struck American observers for more than a generation. When he returned to Russia in 1952 as ambassador, George Kennan noted "the growing inner detachment of the people from the ostensible purpose of a revolutionary regime—their curious lack of interest in the professed ideological inspiration of those who commanded their obedience." There is much homage to Marx in the Soviet Union today but little study of Marxism. Marxist analysis is the province of philosophical institutes where professors write for one another. Ritualistic references to Marx and Lenin appear regularly in the speeches of Soviet leaders, but the sacred writs are used to bless policy, not to shape it. "Revolutionary ideology is the Soviet version of compulsory school prayer," a high-level Soviet specialist in the State Department puts it, "and it plays about the same role." I remember telling a Soviet official about the popular excitement a visitor could still sense in Cuba—brigades of old people, workers, children, all volunteers, fixing up a park at night to "build the revolution"—and eliciting a wistful response, "It was like that here once a long time ago."

Ideology, nevertheless, plays a crucial political role, United States Embassy officials in Moscow argue. It is the sole source of legitimacy for the Kremlin's rule over its continental empire. At some point in the next decade Russians in the Soviet Union will be outnumbered. By some accounts, more than 50 percent of the entire population is already made up of separate ethnic minorities—Ukrainians, Uzbeks, Armenians and others. The "national question" has plagued Soviet leadership from the revolution. They have tried to make a nation of fifteen different peoples, each with its own language, many of different races. The justification for keeping the results of nine centuries of czarist conquest together in one political unit is not nationalism but socialism. As heirs of Lenin and Stalin, the leaders of the Soviet Communist party have authority. As heirs of the czars they have only power. With their ideological credentials challenged by the Chinese, by the Romanians, by the Italian Communist party, the base of the legitimacy on which that power rests becomes shakier. The old debate among Soviet specialists about whether the Soviet Union is more like a cause than a country is giving way to a new consensus. The leaders of the Soviet Union face a crisis of authority. The Kremlin has been forced to admit that there are many roads to socialism and that it does not have all the ideological answers. But if Italians and even Romanians are, to some extent, able to find their own road to socialism and to resist Russification, why shouldn't the Latvians, the Ukrainians, and the Uzbeks be able to do the same? It is not uncommon to find analysts of the Soviet Union who predict the breakup of the Soviet Union before the end of the century.

But the decline of ideology in the Soviet Union brings little comfort to the State Department Sovietologists. Helmut Sonnenfeldt has articulated a new theory which is typical of the new orthodoxy. He has stood John Foster Dulles on his head. The Soviet Union is a threat not because it is the embodiment of an ideology but because it has lost its ideology. We are just entering the era of Soviet imperialism, he told an audience at the Naval War College. For the first time their ambitions go beyond the Eurasian land mass. They are defining their interests in global terms. They are aiding guerrilla movements in Africa and selling airplanes to Peru. Unlike the British and French empires of the nineteenth century or the

American empire, Sonnenfeldt argues, the Russians do not have a civilization that anybody wants. Their model of bureaucratic socialism is not admired. There is little interest anywhere outside of Russia itself in their language or their culture. They have little chance of extending their power by launching a "*mission civilisatrice*" or accepting some new version of the white man's burden. The sole source of their expanding power is military might. Because they are "unable to transplant their values" they seek to maintain their influence through arms.

The Soviet Union, Sonnenfeldt says, is "a younger power with the elemental strength" of an unsophisticated society. The cosmopolitans are gone, killed off in the great purges or stigmatized as dissidents and kept from power. Russian civilization is cruder than American civilization, but it also is less decadent, and therein lies its strength. The Kissinger image of the U.S.-Soviet confrontation reflects these views. It is based on a recurring historical myth—an old society being overtaken by the new, Rome succumbing to the barbarians. The new image of the enemy is probably closer to reality than the exaggerated image of the cold-war years— Hitler in the Kremlin masterminding global subversion. The old image fitted perfectly with the intoxicating vision of an American Century that prevailed in the first cold-war generation. The new image reflects the Spenglerian pessimism of the second: communism may have lost its power to compel belief, but the United States, though still a number one nation, and the West as a whole are in a process of steady and irreversible decline.

The Soviet image of the United States has gone through many changes too in the last sixty years. The United States has held a fascination for Soviet leaders, who have envied American technology and wealth and have feared the ideological power advanced capitalism has been able to exert in the world. Priests of an ideology that affirms the moral and practical superiority of another social system, Soviet leaders have, nonetheless, been beset by feelings of inferiority. These feelings are rooted in Russian history. The national self-image promoted by the great modernizers, from Peter the Great to Stalin, was built on shame for her backwardness, fear for her vulnerability to endless foreign invasions, and self-pity for being bypassed by the main currents of European civilization. "You are a creative society. We are an uncreative society," a prominent member of the Central Committee recently told an American official. The national inferiority complex, to which almost every American diplomat who has negotiated with the Russians sooner or later alludes, has been powerfully and

deliberately reinforced by the snubs and condescension of Western statesmen. Khrushchev describes John Foster Dulles in his memoirs as having
"a physical revulsion against the Soviet Union." The Russians, President
Truman told Henry Wallace, as the latter recorded in his memoirs, "were
like people from across the tracks whose manners were very bad." The
politicians in the Kremlin were "like bulls in a China shop," Truman told
another visitor in May 1945. Their system was only twenty-five years old.
The United States was over one hundred, and the British were centuries
older. "We've got to teach them how to behave."

In the Stalin years the smugness and hostility of Western leaders were
continually reinforced by Soviet suspicion and boorishness. Kennan's
account of his freeze-out in Moscow when he was there briefly as ambassador in 1952 (buggings, provocations, slander in the press, snubs) helps
to explain why American diplomats were contemptuous and condescend-
ing in dealing with the Soviets. (Kennan himself was declared *persona non
grata* and barred from returning to the U.S.S.R. after commenting in
Germany that "the treatment we receive in Moscow is just about like the
treatment we internees received . . . when I was interned here in Germany
for several months during the last war.") Contempt has been an effective
weapon of anti-Soviet policy from the time of the revolution. When
Khrushchev was invited to Camp David for private talks with President
Eisenhower in 1960 (the first Soviet leader to be received in America) he
sensed a calculated slight. "I was suspicious . . . I couldn't for the life of
me find out what this Camp David was . . . Our foreign ministry didn't
know what it was either." (The incident says something about the effec-
tiveness of intelligence services.) Khrushchev, recalling that in the early
days of the revolution a Soviet delegation was invited to a place called
Princes Islands, where "stray dogs were sent to die," was afraid that the
Camp David invitation might be a similar way of showing contempt. "I'm
a little bit ashamed," he writes. "It shows how ignorant we were in some
respects."

In the first twenty-five years of the Russian Revolution, Britain, not the
United States, was the chief antagonist. For Stalin, Roosevelt was a capi-
talist reformer with a relatively progressive and naïve world outlook. (The
President's statement at Yalta that the United States would withdraw
American troops from Europe within two years of victory must have puz-
zled him in light of his own views. "This war is not as in the past," Stalin
told Milovan Djilas, then a high Yugoslav official, two months after Yalta.
"Whoever occupies a territory also imposes on it his own social system

. . . as far as his army can reach. It can not be otherwise.") Stalin saw Churchill, on the other hand, as a classic imperialist who made it clear what a limited role he had in mind for the Soviet Union in building the postwar world. Later Stalin developed the thesis in his *Economic Problems of Socialism* that the "contradictions within the imperialist camp" would eventually lead to a war among capitalist countries, a development he considered to be far more likely than a war between the United States and the Soviet Union. Whether the published thesis reflected his real views—there is evidence that by the early 1950s his fear of war with the United States was growing—we do not know. The only firsthand accounts of conversations with Stalin from this period reveal consistently cautious attitudes about provoking the United States and an enormous respect for American strength. The thesis of a capitalist Armageddon was a convenient piece of official eschatology. The imperialists would destroy each other and the Soviet Union would pick up the pieces and build the new socialist order. It was the Soviet counterpart of the American thesis that the Soviet Union would "mellow" or break up under the relentless pressure of a united capitalist world.

By the end of the war it was clear enough that the United States would emerge as the principal antagonist, taking over Britain's role as dominant economic power and her imperial responsibilities as they slipped from her grasp. At the end of the war the dean of Soviet economists, Eugene Varga, was reprimanded by Stalin for dissenting from the conventional wisdom, shared by Soviet ideologues and American economists alike, that the United States was heading for a major depression. It was an important argument for Stalin, not because he believed the "crisis of capitalism" would lead to an early collapse of American power but because he thought the decline of the domestic market would induce the Americans to sell desperately needed technology to the Soviet Union, just as in the 1930s. When the U.S. economy refused to behave according to the grim predictions, the Soviets adjusted their view of American capitalism and maintained it consistently for more than a generation.

In the recent recession Soviet America watchers refused to share the pessimism of the U.S. commentators about where the economy was heading. They believe that American capitalism is resilient and capable for the foreseeable future of making the necessary structural reforms to permit continued growth. In the Institute for Study of the U.S.A. and in the Institute for the Study of the World Economy there is undisguised admiration for the U.S. economy. Yuri Bobrakov, head of the economics department of the Institute for the Study of the U.S.A., thinks that the United States will make substantial progress on the unemployment problem and avoid serious inflation. He puts great faith in technological innovation. His pro-America conditioning, he says, goes back to his childhood in the thirties. The hero of a Russian children's book he remembers was a young American named Jack who came to a Soviet collective farm and showed them how to be efficient and get rid of their bedbugs. V. Sherchnev, the deputy director of the institute and a well-known economist, believes that, contrary to Soviet propaganda in the past, American industrialists would like to convert from military to nonmilitary production, and that there are no great problems standing in the way. His study of U.S. war industries, he said, had shaken some preconceptions. "It turns out that they are not as profitable as we had thought. Also we have statements from many heads of munitions companies saying they don't like making weapons and would like to find something else to do." When I suggested that that was probably true, but that conversion was an enormous problem because of the dependence of entire communities on weapons contracts, the absence of alternative job opportunities, and the rising unemployment rate, he seemed puzzled at my pessimism. Whether the new optimism about the conversion of war industries—which is not widely shared in the United States by those who have studied the problem—is merely wishful thinking or a piece of calculated ideological revisionism to support the current optimistic line about the possibilities of ending the arms race we do not know.

The official line on the United States has changed even more abruptly and more often than the official line in America on the Soviet Union. During the war Soviet propaganda included a good deal of praise for the great capitalist ally in the fight against Hitler, but no mention, except briefly at the hour of victory, of the billions of dollars of Lend-Lease. Stalin's speech of February 9, 1946, marked so abrupt a change in tone that Supreme Court Justice William O. Douglas called it the "declaration of World War III." In the late forties and early fifties the image of the United States projected by Soviet propagandists was savage. True, there was more substance to some of the Soviet charges than most Americans believed at the time: the United States was indeed "aggressive"—violating Soviet air space, sending in propaganda balloons, and trying to foment insurgencies in the Ukraine and elsewhere. The campaign to surround the Soviet Union was proceeding, and some generals and other high officials in the Truman administration openly talked of preventive war.

But the only picture of the United States presented to Soviet citizens was that of a corrupt, evil, militarist society that worshiped money and oppressed blacks. I remember a children's book of that period in which a fifteen-year-old Southern belle was given a Browning automatic rifle by her father for Christmas to use against the local Negroes. (Some of the American comic-strip caricatures of the Soviet Union in this period were scarcely less inflammatory, although most U.S. propaganda of this sort came from the private sector, not the government, and tended to concentrate on the machinations of Soviet officials rather than young girls.)

Soviet officials in private point to the cease-fire in vicious propaganda as a sign of seriousness about détente. With the thaw after Stalin's death, the tone of anti-American propaganda had already become less strident, but the dramatic changes in the official Soviet image of the United States did not come until 1972. Members of the Institute for the Study of the United States, which U.S. Embassy officials refer to as "the détente establishment," give lectures around the Soviet Union on the virtues of coexistence with the United States. "It was hard to convince people that we could do business with the United States and maintain peaceful relations after all they had been told about your country, but they are now learning."

There is a skeptical view among veteran national security managers such as Paul Nitze that neither academic studies, no matter how insightful or objective they may be, nor professional journals have much impact on Soviet perceptions of the United States. "They don't believe what they read in our newspapers. They believe what they steal." Professor Arbatov may write speeches for Brezhnev, but it is not the "détente establishment" that produces the official perceptions of the United States; it is rather the KGB transmitting its conspiratorial views, conspiratorially obtained, directly into the Chairman's ear. There is something to all this. The KGB is an immense and well-funded bureaucracy. Its major task—not a small one—is to keep the Soviet Union under surveillance, and dissidents and potential troublemakers under control. A secondary task is to try to find out what the United States is up to. It is a commonplace that the Soviets have an easy time finding out what goes on in the "open society" and that their problem is not too little information but too much. Herbert Scoville, former deputy director of the CIA, takes a skeptical view of this. For the sort of information the Soviets want, the United States is not an open society. Political intentions of the President and his advisers, particularly in sensitive areas of the greatest interest to the KGB, are not telegraphed in advance. Kissinger's China trip in 1971 is an example. Both countries are continuing major efforts to procure such information by clandestine means, but these efforts appear to be increasingly unrewarding.

Nikita Khrushchev was the one top Soviet leader who ever expressed himself freely in the West about spies. He told Allen Dulles, then head of the CIA, that his agency should swap reports with the KGB since they were paying the same agents anyway. When he visited the Iowa farmer Roswell Garst and marveled at his hybrid corn, he demanded to know why the Soviet Union didn't have such superior strains. Garst told him it had all been described in several agricultural journals, and Khrushchev snorted, "You should have kept it secret and then I would have found out."

In the war between the KGB and U.S. intelligence agencies each side has had its share of minor triumphs. The Soviet triumphs have been more dramatic. In the early postwar days a Soviet agent, Kim Philby, actually helped organize the CIA as a member of British intelligence. General Gehlen's German intelligence operation, with which the CIA was also working, was penetrated by Soviet agents as well. The U.S. Embassy in Moscow, including the code room, was bugged. A Colonel Whelan attached to the office of the Joint Chiefs of Staff became a Soviet agent. The most valuable spy for the United States was Colonel Oleg Penkovsky, who was highly placed in Soviet military circles. After he was discovered and shot in 1963 the CIA fabricated his memoirs and published them widely as a way of taunting the Soviets and doing a bit of advertising for the clandestine services.

The most secret thing about spying is the effect it all has on perceptions and policies. Even when spies are caught or codes are broken, it is rare that we know the consequences. When I asked a senior U.S. intelligence official whether he could think of an instance in which clandestinely procured intelligence had changed policy, he had trouble recalling any. Penkovsky, who stole military manuals by the dozen and thereby provided employment for hundreds of U.S. analysts, did convey the important information that the Soviets had virtually no operational intercontinental missiles at the time of the Cuban missile crisis. It helped the Pentagon decide that the reason the U-2 flights had been unable to find missiles to photograph was that there weren't any. In 1953, so speculates the official damage report prepared after the bugging of the Moscow code room was discovered, the Soviets learned that Eisenhower was serious about escalating the Korean war, and was leaning toward the use of nuclear weapons if the Soviets did not promptly force the Koreans to settle. They settled.

The compromise of our sensitive secrets, the report concluded, probably served American foreign policy objectives.

Today it is much harder to break codes. The use of the "one-time pad" system means that the codes are changed automatically every day. According to the cryptographic expert David Kahn, it is now impossible to break them. The United States and the Soviet Union, while able to place agents in high places in third countries, are unable to penetrate each other's inner sanctums. The United States and the Soviet Union now get most of their clandestine intelligence about each other from satellites and "communications intercepts," the polite bureaucratic term for bugging. Satellites are no longer really a form of clandestine intelligence collection since both countries acknowledge their existence. Indeed, the SALT agreements are premised on their operation, and each side specifically undertakes not to conceal missile sites, so that they can be monitored by orbiting cameras. There is a great deal of raw information collected by communications intercepts. Such work keeps an entire agency busy—the National Security Agency, which is, indeed, the largest of the U.S. intelligence services.

This agency has been successful in putting bugs in high places, even in the Kremlin limousines. Analysts who have listened to the tapes of these conversations say they are useful for learning somewhat more about the personalities of Soviet leaders but not much else. Typical of one such limousine conversation is the heavy joke. On one occasion Podgorny and Kosygin talk about an African leader who is coming to visit Moscow. They can't remember where he's from or why he has come and they are reduced to giggles. Soviet leaders, like their American counterparts, assume that when they are talking on open lines they can be overheard and they usually act accordingly. It is not likely that the Soviets learn much about U.S. intentions from bugging telephones.

The intelligence services in both the United States and the Soviet Union function in remarkably similar ways. Academic analysts and espionage agents inject their respective biases into the policy-making process in both countries. Scholars at the Institute for the Study of the United States are in much the same position as scholars at the Harvard Russian Research Center or at the Columbia Institute of Russian Studies. The Soviet scholars are of course part of the Soviet Government, which funds their institute, and the American scholars do not normally receive funds from the U.S. Government. But the difference is less than one might think. The American institutes are training schools for the intelligence agencies and the foreign service. Leading scholars, such as Marshall Shulman, play a continuing role as adviser to top officials on Soviet affairs, much as Georgi Arbatov does in the U.S.S.R. There is more independence and diversity at the American institutions, but they are not immune from political pressures. Recently Donald Kendall offered to raise a considerable sum for the Columbia Institute provided no Soviet dissidents would be welcomed there.

Academic analysts in both countries carry on a complex love affair with their subject. Americanologists from Moscow find the United States exotic and seductive, its wickedness altogether fascinating. The Americanologists are a newer breed—the Institute for the Study of the United States started only eight years ago—than their counterparts and so reflect somewhat less the cold-war climate in which Russian studies were organized in the immediate postwar period. Some of the influential early scholars of the Soviet Union in postwar America were disillusioned radicals or former employees of the Office of Strategic Services. They hated the Soviet system but were fascinated by it, and they were captivated by Russia, the culture, the tragic history, and above all the people. (Two recent books, one by the correspondent of the Washington *Post* and the other by the correspondent of *The New York Times,* both of whom lived in the Soviet Union several years, offer a glimpse of the strange attraction the place exerts on those who try to understand it. Both books describe the corruption, inefficiency, cruelty, and naïveté that abound under the Soviet system, yet each is warmly pro-Russian.)

The clandestine mentality is quite different. The CIA and the KGB have the same conspiratorial world view, and the *Weltanschauung* of the spy has the same effect on official perceptions in both countries. If it is worth committing larceny and even murder to get information about a country, then by definition the country is sufficiently depraved to justify the operation. Information procured at great risk and expense will tend to confirm that the target deserved what it got.

Nevertheless, most intelligence reports, analysts say, are ignored. As the Pentagon Papers showed, the CIA prepared reasonably accurate accounts of the origin and character of the National Liberation Front in South Vietnam and its relationship to other political forces, but these never had much impact on the President and his top advisers because conclusions ran counter to their prejudices. According to the Select Committee on Intelligence, factual accounts of what was happening in Chile under Allende were ignored by Nixon and Kissinger for similar reasons. Intelligence analysts complain that particularly under Kissinger careful reports

based on a painstaking compilation of data were never read, while a titil-
lating but meaningless fragment of a bugged conversation or the confes-
sions of a secret agent could always get a hearing in the secretary's office.
They are confident that the same thing is happening in the Kremlin.

Under détente, there are increased opportunities for agents to penetrate
places they have never been before. Virtually every U.S. delegation to the
SALT talks, cultural exchange talks, scientific cooperation talks, and
every other major contact includes a representative of the CIA, and, one
assumes, every Soviet delegation has an agent of the KGB. Secret agents
know each other and even exchange information on a professional basis.
The FBI is worried that the increased mobility of Soviet diplomats and
commercial representatives provides greater opportunities to recruit agents
in the United States. The CIA made available to John Barron for his book
KGB the text of what purports to be a KGB recruiting manual, with in-
structions on how to find Americans who will provide secret information
"on the military and political plans of the U.S. government; on new discoveries and inventions in science and technology; on the work of American intelligence and counterintelligence organs; and on the activities of
international organizations—the UN and others—which are located in the
United States." Soviet agents continue their efforts to buy industrial secrets
and government position papers. Periodically they are discovered and ex-
pelled. In the 1950s agents of the two intelligence services used to kill one
another periodically. A gentlemen's agreement has been in effect for some
years not to do that. The United States used to conduct extensive black
propaganda operations inside the Soviet Union—broadcasts from outside
transmitters disguised as coming from the battleground of guerrilla movements within Soviet territory. The purpose was to foment uprisings, but
this sort of troublemaking has been curtailed in recent years. The "back-
alley war," as Dean Rusk used to call it, has shifted from the home countries, which are reasonably impervious to such activities, and from Europe,
on which both intelligence services concentrated in the immediate postwar
period, to the Third World, where coups are easy to stage, politicians easy
to buy, and secret information is manufactured for sale.

For the Soviets it is more practical to buy technology than to steal it.
Despite the national security restrictions that still limit East-West trade,
the Soviets stand to gain more from a gradual buildup of their technical
base with the help of foreign technology than from espionage. Elaborate
efforts at spying continue, but in some areas, despite enormous devotion of
resources, they still lag behind the United States in certain aspects of mili-

tary technology. The late-model MIG that was flown by a defector to Japan in 1976 turned out to be surprisingly primitive compared with the latest American aircraft and in other respects remarkably advanced.

For the United States the motivation for spying on the Soviet Union is changing somewhat. The strongest argument for taking risks to penetrate the Iron Curtain used to be that there was no other way to get information about the Soviet Union. In 1939 the entire Soviet census was published as one page in *Pravda*. About the time the Soviet population hit 200,000,000, in the middle 1950s, detailed census data began to be published. Although military expenditures are still secret, a great deal of economic data is now publicly available. U.S. Africa and Asia specialists can now see their counterparts in the Soviet foreign ministry. U.S. diplomats are invited to a variety of seminars at the U.S.A. Institute. An M.I.T. political science professor, Lincoln Bloomfield, has arranged political games in Moscow along the lines of those customarily played at the Pentagon. In a recent game on the Middle East, Anatoly Gromyko, the son of the foreign minister and a diplomat himself, played Sadat.

The cold war is a history of mutually reinforcing misconceptions. In the United States ignorance about the Soviet Union produced a good deal of ideological scholarship about the Soviet system which did nothing to discourage Soviet analysts of the United States from giving expression to their own ideological biases about the American way of life. Official stereotypes in both societies have been the foundation stone on which to build solid academic careers. The picture of Stalin's Russia, a much too simple picture at that, haunted American specialists on Soviet affairs for much of the last generation and still continues to dominate scholarly and journalistic thinking. In the critical period of the 1950s Soviet studies perpetuated a static, pessimistic view of Russia as a new form of oriental despotism and missed the fresh currents that were already flowing because, as Professor Alexander Dallin of Stanford University notes, no one ever "incurred a risk to his professional reputation by taking a hard line—even if later such a posture proved to be unwarranted."

Today, according to Marshall Shulman, now adviser on Soviet affairs to the Secretary of State, "what isn't sufficiently understood or appreciated in this country is that the political life of the Soviet Union involves a very rich and complex spectrum. . . . There are people who are involved in the system and yet are critical of it in one way or another. . . . There are many forces for change which are not sufficiently appreciated in this country. . . ." Professor William Zimmerman of the University of Michigan complains that some of his most distinguished fellow-academics still fall into the trap of disposing of the Soviet Union with topic sentences left over from the Stalin period. Richard Pipes calls the Soviet regime "a government devoid of any popular mandate" and Hans J. Morgenthau writes that it "has to rely primarily on nothing but deception and terror" to maintain its rule. Deception, terror, and repression are clearly instruments of rule, but such sweeping statements involve a lack of analysis of the sources of legitimacy of the regime. The preoccupation with Soviet repression perpetuates some myths, such as the notion that the state allocates all jobs. "Job choice is not totally defined by the state," Professor Zimmerman notes; for example, "it remains difficult for Moscow to get people to work in the far north—even though substantial bonuses are offered for accepting such assignments." (There is also a popular myth that the Soviet system is a totally command economy that does not use material incentives.)

Discussion of the Soviet Union in the United States has been so suffused with cold-war ideology that it has been hard to put Soviet reality in perspective. In the light of professions of "socialist legality," Soviet attacks on dissidents are shocking. Yet, compared with many military dictatorships around the world with which the United States has had close friendly relations, the treatment of dissent is lenient. Judged by their own puritanical and egalitarian ideology, the system of privileges now available to the party elite is a betrayal of socialism. Compared with the privileges and trappings of office and opportunities for personal enrichment at the pinnacle of power in most countries, including the United States, the caviar, dachas, and extra Rolls Royces are modest emoluments. Observations of this sort are rarely heard in the United States because they sound or can be made to sound apologetic. But trying to compare the Soviet experience with corruption and repression elsewhere does not mean that scholars, journalists, and activists should defend or rationalize Soviet policy. Too often, however (except for brief moments of official euphoria during the war), analysis of Soviet reality has seemed guided by an impulse to demonstrate that the Soviet Union is a miserable society and a dangerous one. The mythic image of the Soviet Union cultivated by scores of scholars, diplomats, and journalists over the last generation is curiously contradictory: On the one hand, the Russians are astride the world; on the other, their society is one in which "nothing works."

If American analyses of the Soviet Union have been tendentious during the cold war, Soviet analyses of the United States have often been ferocious. In the late 1940s typical studies were entitled *The American*

Gestapo and *The Fascization of American Political Life.* No economic studies could fail to talk of "reactionary manipulators of Wall Street," the "monopolies" and so on. "Every Marxist work on the economics of capitalist countries," *Pravda* declared in September 1950, "must be a bill of indictment." There is still a good deal of outrageous reporting and analysis. Gennadii Vasilkev of *Pravda* recently reported that it is quite common under the American free enterprise system for babies to be sold like commodities. There are also great pools of ignorance even among specialists on the United States. When I asked a young researcher at the Institute for the Study of the U.S.A. how many members of the American Communist party there were, his answer was 200,000! But there has been remarkable progress in sophistication and objectivity in analyzing the United States. Much of the new tone and new intellectual bite in analysis of the United States is attributable to the Institute for the Study of the U.S.A. and the related magazine *U.S.A.,* which now has 35,000 subscribers. A book on U.S. presidents written by one of the senior staff has sold over 400,000 copies. Classic rhetoric is being moderated. "Capitalists" are now referred to as "entrepreneurs" or "managers." The "financial circles" behind U.S. policies have become "bankers." What Frederick Starr of the Kennan Institute calls "the Soviet rediscovery of America" has occurred through many small steps—specialized studies on Congress, on the economy, on the civil rights movement, students, the scientific establishment, and so on. A. N. Melnikov's *Contemporary Class Structure of the U.S.A.* for example, based on census returns, is a nonideological analysis of social strata in America. It notes that workers are not a "solid undifferentiated mass," nor are they near revolt. Soviet journalists traveling in the United States now write objective, even sympathetic portraits of their encounters with American life. Accounts of the cold war are more moderate. ("Colossal distrust was built up on both sides.") There is even veiled criticism of the KGB's role in the past and of Lysenko and intellectual conformity, all of which, it is said, fed anticommunism in the West.

But much of the analysis is like a slightly blurred photograph. Professor Robert Byrnes of the University of Indiana, who has spent a good deal of time on academic exchanges, thinks that Soviet scholars lack the feel for "what makes us tick," that even after spending a year in America, "they work on a mental frequency that will just not pick up American signals." There is a certain smugness about such observations, as if American Sovietologists understand what makes the Russians tick. The reality is that both sets of scholars and journalists operate under enormous handicaps which are reflected in their results. It is no doubt accurate to say that Soviet specialists are now getting more of the facts—though there are still great gaps—but missing the truth. Part of the explanation is that much of the scholarship is instrumental—to support some official preconception on which policy is grounded. Partly, the reason is that there are ideological limits within which scholars must work. Travel to the United States, which is an indispensable professional perquisite, may be denied a scholar who displays an unseemly sympathy for his subject or strays from the ideological path.

Nevertheless, the picture that emerges from Soviet studies is of a strong America with an economy powerful enough to withstand its "internal contradictions" for years to come, of a social system that has successfully withstood the traumas of Watergate and Vietnam, and of an elite who are formidable ideological opponents yet sober and responsible statesmen with whom it is possible to do business.

CHAPTER 5
The Deadly Entanglement

"The single most important component of our policy toward the Soviet Union," Henry Kissinger told the Senate Foreign Relations Committee on September 19, 1974, "is the effort to limit strategic weapons competition." The test of the new relationship with the Soviet Union—whether it is really new and whether it is really "mutually advantageous"—is in the arena where the most vital interests of the two powers are at stake. No matter how many ballet companies are exchanged or how much Pepsi is drunk in Odessa, the perceptions of the roomful of American and Soviet officials in charge of defining the relationship are not likely to mellow as long as more megaton weapons, each having at least two hundred times the destructive power of the "Fat Man" that was dropped on Hiroshima, continue to be aimed at one another. (At the beginning of 1977 the United States had about 9,000 of such warheads aimed at the Soviet Union, and the Soviets had about 3,500 aimed at the United States.)

Arms controllers like to talk about the "mad momentum" of the arms race, to use former Secretary of Defense Robert McNamara's words, almost as if it were a natural disaster. Kissinger defended the Vladivostok agreements with the Soviet Union for limiting strategic delivery vehicles (bombers, intercontinental missiles) to 2,400 on both sides as a way of putting a "cap" on the arms race—a sort of U.S.-Soviet alliance against the forward thrust of technology. But plumbing metaphors are not much help either. The arms race is not perceived by those who keep it going as a spurting water main. Both sides see the nuclear stockpiles not merely as a danger but also as their best source of security. After thousands of hours of negotiations the American elite and the Soviet elite think more alike on arms issues than they did ten years ago. Americans have educated their Soviet counterparts in the arcane doctrines of nuclear war and preparation for war.

One of the few reassuring myths of the cold war was that the Soviet leaders would learn from experience and in the process "become more like us." The pressure to husband resources to produce consumer goods and to manage an advanced technologically dependent society would force even old Bolsheviks to abandon their revolutionary visions and to become pragmatic and responsible. "Convergence," the term invented by Kremlinologists to describe the narrowing of the ideological gap between the two societies, would make it possible to do business with the Kremlin. Two "status quo" powers, each looking at the world increasingly in the same way, each desiring much the same things, could come to terms on the ground rules for coexistence.

But, for the most part, convergence has complicated the arms negotiation process. The more both sides have come to think alike about military technology and military doctrine the harder it has been to strike bargains that actually inhibit military power. The military establishments on both sides subscribe to the same two basic principles: (1) "Don't negotiate when you are behind. Why accept a permanent position of number two?" and (2) "Don't negotiate when you are ahead. Why accept a freeze in an area of military competition where the other side has not kept up with you?" Twenty years ago the situation was different. The Soviet Union would make sweeping disarmament proposals, condemn arms-control measures to moderate but not end the weapons race as "tricks to deceive public opinion," and refuse to admit the technical problems of verifying that weapons stockpiles had indeed been destroyed. There was, to be sure, a fundamental reluctance on both sides to trust disarmament as an alternative strategy for achieving security. Well publicized disarmament negotiations served political purposes. For the Soviet Union the "struggle for peace" became a worldwide campaign to convince millions of people that the United States posed a threat of nuclear war. In the late 1940s the Stockholm peace appeal was a major diplomatic weapon. For the United States the negotiations were largely defensive, aimed at "shifting the onus" for failure of the talks, as the State Department lingo of the time put it, to the Soviets. Neither side expected anything to come of the elaborate charade. Proposals were modified from time to time just enough to intrigue the public and to confuse the press.

In the late 1950s American arms controllers began educating their Soviet counterparts. Scientists met each other at Pugwash meetings, the informal exchanges on nuclear issues begun at the Nova Scotia home of Cleveland industrialist Cyrus Eaton. A small group of U.S. economists and systems analysts had developed a body of theory about deterrence and a specialized vocabulary—"first strike," "second strike," "stability," "accidental war," "counterforce," "countervalue"—and these they began to teach the Soviet scientists and military officers who showed up for the "nonofficial" discussions. Soon articles in Soviet journals began to reflect the new knowledge and the new vocabulary. Veteran participants in arms-control discussions say there is a lag of about five years before they hear their own ideas coming back at them from the Soviet side. An international "arms-control community" developed. (A number of the Pugwash regulars became senior officials of the Kennedy administration.) By the mid-1960s the emphasis in official Soviet proposals began to shift from disarmament to arms control. The difference is fundamental. The idea of disarmament is that both sides agree to reduce their capability to make war on each other. The theory of arms control is that both sides try to make the military environment safer—by eliminating particularly dangerous weapons, reducing the danger of accidental war, cutting costs by eliminating weapons that both sides would prefer not to build, or removing the temptation of either side to "preempt" a nuclear war by starting one.

When the SALT I agreement was signed in Moscow on May 26, 1972, Kissinger's speech writer, Winston Lord, wrote a sentence that became part of Nixon's message to Congress and, in slightly altered form, a standard piece of campaign rhetoric a few months later. "Never before have two adversaries, so deeply divided by conflicting ideologies and political rivalries, been able to limit the armaments on which their survival depends." Yet five years later the arsenals on both sides were larger and deadlier than before.

The SALT negotiations have been used by the superpowers to improve their military capabilities. Within a week of the signing of SALT I, Secretary of Defense Melvin Laird and John S. Foster, Jr., director of Defense Research and Engineering, proposed to the Senate Appropriations Committee and the House Armed Services Committee a "series of SALT related adjustments to strategic programs" including the Trident submarine and ULMS (undersea long-range missile systems), new bases for bombers, the B-1 bomber, the controversial supersonic replacement for the B-52, improved warheads, communication systems, and other improvements.

The Defense Department argued that all these improvements were necessary to provide a "timely and credible hedge" against the possibility that the Soviets would abrogate the agreement or fail to renew it. (SALT I was an interim agreement that expires in October 1977.) The Soviet Union has continued to build up its missile force as well. The Vladivostok agreements reached in 1974 called for limiting both sides to 2,400 "delivery vehicles" (airplanes and missiles capable of reaching the homeland of the other power). Of these, 1,320 could be "MIRVed," that is, outfitted with hydra-like multiple warheads that can be separately aimed at different targets, a way of converting one missile into eight or ten. The Soviet Union is continuing to add to its missile force, although apparently not at the same high rate as in recent years. From 1972 to 1976, according to the secretary of defense, the Soviets added 600 nuclear warheads to their arsenal. In the same period the United States increased its stock of warheads by 3,200.

During the projected period of the SALT II accords, which runs into the mid-1980s, the United States is planning to spend up to $70–$100 billion for additional strategic nuclear weapons systems including the Trident submarine, the cruise missile, and new warheads of increasing accuracy. The Soviet Union, according to CIA analysts, may well spend more than that. Under the 1974 agreement it is quite possible for 29,000 strategic nuclear weapons to be deployed by 1985. Such numerical limitations do not seem especially restrictive, but even these have been used to spur a qualitative arms race. With the numbers fixed, the military advantages of improved missile accuracy, hardening and protection of missile sites, speed and maneuverability become more important. Since no agreement on capping the qualitative arms race has been proposed, both sides are focusing on the growing threat of minor technological breakthroughs that could upset their planning. "Arms control negotiations," Herbert Scoville, Jr., former deputy director of the CIA, observed shortly after SALT I was signed, "are rapidly becoming the best excuse for escalating rather than toning down the arms race."

What, then, has been accomplished by the years of arms negotiations? Perhaps the most impressive achievement was the forestalling of an expensive ABM system. This was a classic case of both sides agreeing not to build something that neither side wanted but that each would have probably ended up building in the absence of an agreement. The United States had experimented, Herbert York, President Eisenhower's director of research and engineering at the Pentagon, recalls, with three generations of antiballistic missile systems at a cost of more than $8 billion.

But none was satisfactory. The Soviet Union, we know now, had had similar discouraging experiences with much more primitive systems. They were ready, therefore, after years of persuasion, to accept a cardinal tenet of American arms-control doctrine, that defensive systems are, contrary to what one might think, worse than offensive systems because they make your adversary think that perhaps you think that you can save your population in a nuclear war and hence you may be tempted to launch one. By the time of SALT I both sides were looking for ways to avoid the unpredictable but staggering cost. In the context of an unlimited arms race, the agreement to build only a token ABM was no mean achievement, but it provided none of the momentum its most enthusiastic proponents claimed for it. Since ABMs stimulate the growth of offensive weapons, each side wishing to ensure that it can destroy the other despite the possibility that many of its missiles may be obliterated in the air, arms controllers hoped that canceling the ABM would put a brake on the buildup of offensive missiles. But it did not happen. The stockpile of nuclear weapons has doubled in the last five years.

One of the pieties of arms control is that one step leads to another. President Kennedy announced the test-ban agreement in 1963 by quoting a Chinese proverb that a journey of a thousand miles begins with a single step. But one step in these bizarre negotiations does not necessarily build the confidence that is supposed to encourage another. The test ban, it was claimed, would inhibit weapons development, but more tests took place underground in the five years after it was concluded than in all the years between 1945 and the date the treaty went into effect. These were the years of the most sophisticated developments in warheads, including MIRV, just as the years since the ABM agreements have been a time of rapid buildup of offensive weapons on both sides. The partial test ban was an effective antipollution device, and the ABM agreement saved money. But neither reduced military capabilities on either side. Such agreements do not build confidence, because they communicate nothing reassuring about the intentions of the other side. The Joint Chiefs of Staff are not persuaded that the Soviet Union is a lesser threat because their generals have agreed not to put nuclear weapons in orbit or in Antarctica (two of the U.S.-Soviet arms-control agreements of the 1960s), since they have no reason to do either no matter how aggressive their intentions might be. Indeed, the elaborate exceptions and caveats that have accompanied every arms-control agreement probably communicate as much about intentions as the agreement itself. The signing of a biological-warfare convention instead of an agreement banning chemical and biological warfare, which had been traditionally discussed together in disarmament negotiations, underscored the reality that the Joint Chiefs of Staff (and probably their Soviet counterparts) had plans for using noxious gases under certain contingencies which they did not want to change. Similarly, the seabed treaty for demilitarizing the ocean floor was written in such a way as to exempt antisubmarine warfare systems that the U.S. Navy did not wish to give up.

The Vladivostok agreement, as a *New York Times* editorial pointed out shortly after the euphoric communiqué announcing it, "appears to be an agreement between the military on both sides—achieved through the intermediaries of the chiefs of government—to permit the buildups each desired . . . If this is 'putting a cap on the arms race,' then a shrimp can whistle—as a former Soviet leader, Nikita Khrushchev, was fond of saying." The Vladivostok numbers, whatever the motivation behind them, neatly accommodate the current building programs of both sides. The Soviets, who are sensitive to widespread criticism that a treaty inviting a buildup is a strange arms-control measure—they have yet to publish the numerical limits in their press—came to Vladivostok with even higher numbers. Both U.S. and Soviet spokesmen defend the agreement by arguing that a high ceiling is better than none at all. But skeptics point out that a ten-year agreement that ends when the projected $100 billion building program on both sides is completed is not a limit at all. Frank Barnaby, director of the Institute of Peace Research in Stockholm, calls the whole thing a fraud.

Whether the SALT talks are a "success" or not depends upon the perspective from which one views them. If you believe that without the agreement, weapons expenditures and weapons stockpiles would have been a great deal higher, then the agreement was important. There is some evidence that this is the case with respect to the ABM. Both sides would probably have gone ahead despite their reservations. But in other areas the agreements codified but did not limit any weapons programs. Neither side had to give up anything except the possibility of building something they had no intention of building anyway. Before the Vladivostok agreement the United States had planned to MIRV 1,046 missiles. President Ford stated publicly that "we do have an obligation to step up to that ceiling" (the 1,320 MIRVed missiles permitted under the Vladivostok agreement). Thus the agreements actually encouraged 274 missiles that might never have been built. Since the Soviets had no operational MIRVed missiles when the agreement was signed, in their case this agreement was a cap for an empty tube that is only now being filled.

Both sides make ritualistic efforts through negotiations to limit weapons programs of the other. In 1973 the Soviets proposed a freeze on new strategic programs including the Trident and the B-1. Eight years earlier the Johnson administration had proposed a similar freeze just as it became apparent that the Soviets were about to go into a huge missile buildup. The initial proposals of the Carter administration, which called for "deep cuts" instead of the high Vladivostok ceilings, would have required the Soviets to cut their heavy land-based missiles from 308 to 150. The effect would have been to force the Soviets to scrap their latest technology and to shift their force to sea-based missiles, systems in which the Soviets are at a distinct technological and geographical disadvantage. The results predictably were the same in all cases. Negotiations cannot succeed in securing important unilateral advantages for either side. What they can do is to provide the military establishments in Washington and Moscow with more reliable information about the other side on which to do their planning. If they are to do more—that is, actually cut back on existing or planned military capabilities—much tougher internal negotiations in both countries must take place.

In his analysis of the SALT negotiations in the British *Journal of International Studies* Milton Leitenberg concludes:

> In the U.S. and in the U.S.S.R., neither the President nor the party Central Committee have been sufficiently interested, or interested at all, in taking on their respective military leadership on the question of the limits of strategic nuclear weapons development. Either they agree with the reasons their military commands want these weapons and in the numbers and kinds in which they want them, or they are afraid to contest the issue.

Military bureaucracies charged with making, servicing, and deploying tens of thousands of nuclear weapons and refining doctrines for their use understandably think of them, as Admiral Arthur Radford, a former chairman of the Joint Chiefs of Staff, put it over twenty years ago, as "conventional weapons." So thoroughly integrated into the striking forces of the United States are nuclear weapons that when the Johnson administration decided to commence bombing of North Vietnam in 1965 neither the navy nor the air force had any plans for such an attack that did not involve atomic explosives. A rapid buildup in conventional explosives was

ordered, but the politically unusable nuclear weapons were never with-
drawn. The use of nuclear weapons, despite the widespread understanding
of the grave implications of such use, is the foundation of U.S. military
doctrine. A few months before he was dismissed by President Ford, Secretary of Defense James Schlesinger made it clear that the United States
under certain circumstances would use nuclear weapons first; the usual
contingency mentioned is a Soviet attack on Western Europe. A brief out-
cry followed from some congressional critics, but Schlesinger defended
himself by pointing out that this had always been U.S. policy. When the
Soviet Union was far behind in nuclear weapons, it used to condemn them
as instruments of genocide. More recently, Soviet statements reflect their
bulging stockpiles. Marshal Viktor Kulikov, writing in *Pravda,* for example, states that "nuclear war could be an instrument of politics."

In both countries leading military bureaucrats constitute a potent political force with which the political leadership must negotiate. No U.S.
President has been prepared to fight for a disarmament measure—or
military budget, for that matter—which left the Joint Chiefs of Staff deeply
unhappy. In the Soviet Union, as we shall explore further, only Khrushchev
was prepared to trust his own instinct enough to ignore the grumbling of
his marshals that he was starving them. He paid for his "harebrained
schemes," of which his parsimony in military matters was one, with dis-
missal and instant obscurity one October day in 1964. The point has not
been lost on Khrushchev's successors, who enlisted the help of the military
in arranging his departure.

The military establishments in the United States and the Soviet Union
are no doubt each other's best allies. The Soviets accommodate Pentagon
budget planners by surfacing submarines, parading a new weapons system in Red Square, or writing bellicose articles in military journals. (Some
congressional doves are convinced of a conspiracy.) Soviet military planners in turn, a Soviet general once told me, feed on the bellicose statements
and extravagant budget projections that emanate from time to time from
the Pentagon. Military bureaucracies, like any other, have a professional
interest in keeping what they have, in enjoying the power and prestige of
being at the frontiers of technology, and in projecting a threat that justifies
bigger budgets. (No market operates here. Threat is the substitute for consumer demand.) But it would be a great mistake to picture the arms race
as a product of a cabal of generals in Washington and Moscow vetoing the
peace plans of the politicians. In fact, the basic assumptions of the arms
race have been shared by the political leadership in Washington and
Moscow since the dawn of the nuclear age.

The political elites who held power in the United States and the Soviet Union when the nuclear age began had learned the same lesson from their wartime experiences about the relationship of military power and peace, for they had had the same teacher. In the United States "Munich" was the symbol for a whole generation of leaders of the failure of the preceding generation, a failure rooted in military weakness and flabby will. For Stalin, betrayal by the only man he had ever trusted reinforced his paranoia. The Soviet Union must "catch up" with the West or once again the long succession of invaders—Tatars, Mongols, Swedes, French, Germans, Poles, Lithuanians—would recommence. In the United States, at a time when Stalingrad (now Volgograd) was still under siege and it would have taken a lively imagination to conjure up a Soviet threat of world domination, U.S. military planners had already drawn the design for a huge postwar military machine. As the war ended, the army demanded a ground force capable of expanding to 4.5 million men within a year. The navy wanted to keep 600,000 men, 371 major combat ships, 5,000 auxiliaries, and a "little air force" of 8,000 planes. The air force insisted on being a separate service with a 70-group force and 400,000 men. With these plans, the top military officers served notice that they did not intend ever again to postpone mobilization until after the diplomats had failed.

But when the war ended in 1945 the United States, despite objections from James Forrestal, Dean Acheson, and other national security managers of the time, began a rapid demobilization of its 12.3-million-man military establishment. The infrastructure acquired in war, the string of new bases, the intelligence networks, military research programs, and military assistance remained, but U.S. ground forces shrank to 670,000 men by 1947. One of the early myths of the cold war was that the Soviet Union, whose forces numbered about 11.3 million at their peak during the war, did not demobilize. Then, as now, military planners in the United States would ask, "Why does the Soviet Union need all those forces? What are they up to?" Indeed, the existence of the large Soviet ground armies was the strongest piece of evidence for the official view that the Soviets might attack West Europe. (In 1950 Winston Churchill proclaimed that but for the American atomic bomb Soviet divisions would already be at the English Channel.)

But in fact the Soviets did demobilize in secret: by 1947 they had approximately 2.8 million men under arms, not a number that would suggest aggressive intentions given the immensity of Soviet territory, the history of invasion, and the Russian tradition of maintaining enormous standing armies. In this as well as in other crucial stages of the arms race the Soviet Union chose to disguise its military weakness. The motive was obviously self-protection. In the early postwar years Soviet military planners published articles announcing that their strategy was to occupy Western Europe in the event the United States dropped the atomic bomb on Soviet territory. The mythical Soviet hordes constituted Stalin's only deterrent. But the effect was to fuel the nuclear-arms race. From the early postwar period, U.S. planners have regarded U.S. nuclear strength as a counterweight to Soviet superiority in conventional forces.

By 1948, postwar rearmament began on both sides. The United States stepped up its production of nuclear weapons, and the Soviet Union, in addition to its crash program to produce the bomb, built up its armed forces to almost five million men by 1953. (Curiously, Western intelligence agencies underestimated this buildup, just as they had grossly overestimated Soviet forces a few years earlier.) The mutually reinforcing buildup reflected the sharp deterioration in the political relations of the two powers. The Soviet Union consolidated its hold on Eastern Europe, challenged the United States over Berlin, and appeared to have launched a war in Korea. The latter event triggered a massive military buildup in the United States and Western Europe, including German rearmament.

In the spring of 1950, just before the Korean invasion, a group of high-level national security officials headed by Paul Nitze completed a review of U.S. defense policy, NSC 68. Only recently declassified, the top-secret document reflects the official apocalypticism of the time:

> The Soviet Union is developing the military capacity to support its design for world domination. The Soviet Union actually possesses armed forces far in excess of those necessary to defend its national territory . . .
>
> Should a major war occur in 1950 the Soviet Union and its satellites are considered by the Joint Chiefs of Staff to be in a sufficiently advanced state of preparation immediately to undertake and carry out the following campaigns:
> To overrun Western Europe . . .
> To launch air attacks against the British Isles . . .
> To attack selected targets with atomic weapons, now including the likelihood of such attacks against targets in Alaska, Canada, and the United States . . .

The CIA, according to NSC 68, predicted that by 1954 the Soviet nuclear-bomb stockpile would reach 200. (The U.S. stockpile was close to 600 at the time.) The writers of NSC 68 warned:

Our intelligence estimates assign to the Soviet Union an atomic bomber capability already in excess of that needed to deliver available bombs . . . For planning purposes, therefore, the date the Soviets possess an atomic stockpile of 200 bombs would be a critical date for the United States, for the delivery of 100 atomic bombs on targets in the United States would seriously damage this country.

The Nitze group recommended "substantial increases" in military spending and warned that "sacrifice and discipline will be demanded of the American people. They will be asked to give up some of the benefits they have come to associate with their freedoms."

Zbigniew Brzezinski, President Carter's national security adviser, has a cyclical theory to explain "how the cold war was played." We are presently in the sixth round of a U.S.-Soviet confrontation, he says, characterized by alternating periods of Soviet assertiveness and U.S. assertiveness. In the first phase, 1945–1947, both sides demobilized. (The United States had fewer than 100 atomic bombs.) Both sides were skirmishing for position, trying to establish the ground rules for sharing power in the postwar world. "The Soviet Union should take the place that is due it and therefore should have bases in the Mediterranean for its merchant fleet," said Foreign Minister Vyacheslav Molotov at the London Foreign Ministers Conference of September 1945. The United States opposed this notion as well as Soviet moves, during this period, to expand its power in Japan, Iran, and Turkey. "Unsettled political and social conditions in the West," Brzezinski concludes, "as well as the Soviet advantage on the ground favored the Soviet Union in the event of hostilities in Europe. The U.S. nuclear monopoly as well as the vastly superior American economy—not to speak of the general exhaustion of the Soviet society—boded ill for the Soviet Union in the event of any protracted conflict." When I asked a Soviet scholar recently why he thought the United States did not use the atomic bomb against the Soviet Union when there was no danger of retaliation in kind, he replied, "American public opinion wouldn't allow it."

In the second phase, 1948–1952, U.S. policy became overtly anti-Soviet and anticommunist: the Truman Doctrine, a counterinsurgency campaign in Greece, the development of bipartisan support for "containment." Despite the U.S.S.R.'s economic weakness—the shattered Soviet economy did not reach its prewar level until 1953, the year of Stalin's death—and the U.S. nuclear monopoly, this was, according to Brzezinski, an "assertive" period of Soviet policy: the Czechoslovak coup, the tightening of Soviet control elsewhere in Eastern Europe, the Berlin blockade, and the

Korean war. Stalin's motivation for the rapid and often brutal consolidation of his empire in Eastern Europe and his challenge to the United States in Berlin was not clear at the time to the American national security elite. The latter operated on what the Pentagon likes to call "worst-case assumption," that these moves were the first stage in a Hitler-like timetable of conquest. The motivation was much more likely defensive. We know now from verbatim conversations between Stalin and leaders of the Italian Communist party in January 1951 that Stalin had come to believe "the danger of general war to be great and imminent."

The third phase (1953–1957) was a period of U.S. initiative, Brzezinski argues. The Korean war had precipitated major rearmament, including a crash program to step up nuclear-weapons production and to deploy them in forward bases in Europe. Stalin's successors, aware of the U.S.S.R.'s relative weakness and lacking the stomach for the brinkmanship Stalin showed in the Berlin blockade, called for détente. "We stand, as we have always stood," said the new premier, Georgi Malenkov, "for the peaceful coexistence of the two systems." A nuclear war would cause universal destruction, he said, departing from the official orthodoxy of the day, which held that capitalism would perish in a nuclear war and communism would triumph. Brzezinski, echoing the views of George Kennan, Adam Ulam, and other students of U.S.-Soviet relations, sees the period following Stalin's death as one of "missed U.S. opportunities." The Americans "failed to capitalize on the political and military momentum generated by the repulsion of Stalin's probes—either by exploiting to its own advantage the surfacing Soviet weakness or by taking advantage of the Soviet interest in détente."

During this period the Soviet Union acquired the hydrogen bomb, actually testing one a few months before the United States did. By 1955 the U.S.S.R. had about 350 bombers that could deliver such bombs on U.S. territory, but the United States had almost four times as many planes capable of delivering nuclear weapons to Soviet territory. This was an era of bloodcurdling Dullesian rhetoric—"massive retaliation," "going to the brink"—but avoidance of confrontation. The United States made considerable use of CIA operations and paramilitary forces in Iran, Guatemala, Indonesia, and elsewhere, but carefully avoided conflict with the Soviet Union. Dulles' failure to intervene in Hungary to protect the freedom fighters of Budapest against Soviet tanks made it clear to Khrushchev, who had succeeded to leadership, that Dulles' policy of "rollback" and "liberation" was just political talk. (Why Brzezinski calls the first Eisenhower term a period of U.S. "assertiveness" is not clear from the case he makes.)

Khrushchev and Dulles were perfect partners. Both were masters of bluster and bluff. The Soviets did what they could to disguise this fact. Although at the time they had fewer than 100 bombers capable of reaching the United States, they convinced the U.S. military that there was actually a "bomber gap" in their favor by ostentatiously displaying a few prototypes at May Day air shows. Sometimes, as former CIA director Allen Dulles has written, they would fly the same squadron of planes in circles to create the impression of a mighty armada, relying on nervous Pentagon officials to make extravagant claims for their performance. A few years later the same partnership of Soviet showmen and an American military audience more than willing to be convinced created a similarly fictitious missile gap.

Soviet scholars today privately criticize Khrushchev's "reckless" resort to nuclear threats and acknowledge that his boast about being able to hit a fly in outer space with his missiles was dangerous because it added fuel to the arms race. Verbal bellicosity, they admit, was a substitute for the nuclear stockpiles Khrushchev was unwilling to spend the money to build. This analysis does not find its way into print.

In the fourth phase (1958–1963), which Brzezinski calls "premature Soviet globalism," Khrushchev became more activist, aiding Sukarno in Indonesia and Castro's revolutionary regime ninety miles from Miami, exerting increased pressure on U.S. forces in Berlin, and proclaiming a global policy of support for "wars of national liberation." In the early fifties, Brzezinski argues, détente was "primarily designed to shore up a threatened status quo," but in the late fifties it was meant to change it.

Khrushchev was a showman and believed in what Dean Acheson once called the shadows of power, the psychological intangibles that affect statesmen, such as prestige, awe, dread. In the late fifties he acted as if he believed that the "correlation of forces" had shifted to the Soviet Union. Euphoria in the "socialist world" was infectious; in late 1957 Mao declared in the Kremlin that "the East Wind prevails over the West Wind." Khrushchev delivered what President Eisenhower took as an ultimatum on Berlin —a separate peace treaty with East Germany would be signed, and the allies would have to get permission from the Germans to keep their troops in Berlin—and he repeated the threat a year later to President Kennedy. Two weeks before Kennedy took office Khrushchev made a tough speech vowing support for national-liberation movements, which the new administration took as a thrown gauntlet. All the while, Khrushchev was drastically cutting Soviet ground troops and adding to the Soviet missile force. At the time the United States and the Soviet Union were each spending about $40 billion a year on defense. The next two years in the United States was a period of rapid arms buildup, a big increase in missiles, counterinsurgency forces, and ground forces, for fighting—according to official Pentagon doctrine—"two and one-half wars simultaneously."

The first two years of the Kennedy era was a time of perpetual confrontation—the Bay of Pigs, the frosty encounter in Vienna, the Berlin crisis of 1961, the resumption of nuclear testing in the atmosphere, and finally the missile crisis of October 1962. What was Khrushchev attempting? The most plausible explanation of Khrushchev's decision to put intermediate-range missiles in Cuba is that the Soviet leader was seeking to compel recognition of what in the era of détente is accepted as "the rough equivalence" of U.S. and Soviet power.

At a closed meeting of communist ambassadors held in Washington shortly after the missile crisis Anastas Mikoyan, according to the Hungarian chargé who was present, confirmed that Khrushchev's attempt to turn intermediate-range missiles into the equivalent of intercontinental missiles was designed to overcome the huge U.S. lead without incurring the expense of building additional weapons. The gamble was meant as a prelude to a grand negotiation on Berlin and on limiting arms, but it failed, in Brzezinski's words, because it did not have "a sufficiently dynamic economic foundation or the backing of an adequately developed military technology."

The fifth round in the cold war Brzezinski calls "the cresting of American globalism." Between 1963 and 1968 the United States sent 500,000 troops to Vietnam. North Vietnam, a Soviet ally, was subjected to a rain of bombs that began in the midst of a visit to Hanoi by Soviet premier Kosygin. This was a time of extravagant imperial rhetoric in Washington and extraordinary overconfidence. The projection of American military power in the wake of the Soviet humiliation in Cuba was changing the world balance of power in America's favor. Within two years pro-Soviet leaders around the world—Goulart in Brazil (March 1964), Ben bella in Algeria (June 1965), Papandeou in Greece (July 1965), Nkrumah in Ghana (February 1966), Sukarno in Indonesia (March 1966)—were overthrown, sometimes, as in Brazil and Greece, with a little help from the United States. The U.S. military establishment, which only a few years earlier had warned that the Soviets were determined to achieve military supremacy, now concluded that the Kremlin was resigned to being a permanent underdog. The Soviets had "lost the quantitative race," Secretary McNamara declared in 1965, "and they are not seeking to engage us in that contest. It means there is no indication that the Soviets are seeking to develop a strategic nuclear force as large as ours."

The sixth round, which is still going on, began when the United States discovered that the Vietnam intervention symbolized American weakness rather than strength, and that the Soviet Union had taken advantage of the misadventure to catch up with the United States in military power. In 1965 McNamara estimated that the United States had three or four times the missiles and bombers the Soviets had. Three years later this "superiority" in numbers of missiles was largely erased. By the early 1970s the Soviet Union was actually ahead in missile launchers. The era of détente was officially proclaimed when the American and Soviet elites acknowledged to each other that for practical political purposes the two countries were equal in destructive power. I once showed a high-ranking U.S. general a Soviet statement ascribing détente to the new "correlation of forces" largely brought about by the Soviet missile buildup, and he said he could have written the article himself.

We are now supposed to be in the era of "parity," or "essential equivalence," with respect to military strength, but in truth the military balance is a Platonic ideal that exists inside the heads of professional war planners. The two questions these planners endlessly ask—How much is enough? and Who is ahead?—have no clear, objective answers. It all depends where you start, what sort of an enemy you think you are facing, and what you think you can do with military power. The consensus on arms limitation broke down in the United States about the time Nixon was forced from office. (The Soviets make a good deal of the coincidence in timing.) Paul Nitze, veteran national security manager, resigned publicly from the SALT negotiating team, charging, along with a complaint to the *Wall Street Journal* that the KGB was enticing the American negotiators with beautiful women, that the SALT agreements were endangering national security. Former Secretary of Defense James Schlesinger was dismissed from office a few months later by President Ford because his alarmist picture of the military balance was incompatible with what could be achieved in the arms-control negotiations.

Schlesinger believes that "from the military standpoint the changing international reality is that the United States has been shrinking in terms of its relative power, while the Soviet Union has been growing." This is, of course, a true statement, given the fact that the United States was once

incomparably ahead of the Soviet Union in military power. The real issue
is the significance of the trend.

Schlesinger thinks it ominous that the United States today, despite the
$112 billion military budget, is spending a smaller fraction of the gross
national product on the military than a decade ago. He received an enthusiastic welcome in Peking because of his thesis that the United States
must spend more to maintain a worldwide counterweight to the Soviet
Union. To Schlesinger the "balance" is disappearing, because the Soviets,
even though "behind," have the "momentum," and that somehow can be
translated into political power. The balance rests on the three basic elements of the U.S. and Soviet military establishments: the strategic nuclear
forces (missiles and airplanes that can deliver nuclear bombs to the territory of the other), the navies, and the armies squared off against each other
in central Europe.

The nuclear-arms race is the strangest military competition in history.
Before the nuclear age a nation could calculate its killing power, measure
it against that of its enemy, and make a rational judgment whether to go to
war. To conquer Alsace-Lorraine, for example, was worth so many thousand German soldiers. But such a judgment is impossible in the world of
the atomic bomb because there is no objective that is worth the destruction
of your own society, and the risks of such destruction in what modern-day
strategists blandly call a "nuclear exchange" are very great. Almost fifteen
years ago the Department of Defense pointed out that if 100 nuclear warheads landed on the Soviet Union, 37 million people, or 15 percent of the
population, would die instantly and 59 percent of the industrial capacity
would be destroyed. If 300 such warheads were to land on target, 96
million people would die and 77 percent of the industrial capacity would
be destroyed. It is inconceivable that the present Soviet leadership or any
sane successors would, as McGeorge Bundy, former national security adviser to Presidents Kennedy and Johnson, has pointed out, deliberately
sacrifice ten cities for the purpose of humiliating or blackmailing the
United States. The prospect of "mutual assured destruction" is sufficiently
compelling so that neither side dares to do what each has the physical
power to accomplish. The Soviet Union has five major population centers
and 145 other cities with a population of 100,000 or more. Given these
geographical and psychological realities, a stockpile of 500 nuclear warheads would represent tremendous "overkill" capacity. The U.S. stockpile,
it will be recalled, is now almost 9,000.

No one denies that the United States and the Soviet Union each have more than enough nuclear weapons to blow up the other several times over. Nor does any American strategist—even such advocates of bigger military budgets as Paul Nitze and former Chief of Naval Operations Admiral Elmo Zumwalt—claim that the United States could not respond to a Soviet surprise attack with devastation of the Soviet Union. Even if all the land-based missiles were destroyed in a surprise attack and no bombers reached their target, the nuclear-missile submarine fleet would survive. There is no way to target the submerged submarines with confidence, because most of them cannot be found. The United States has 41 such submarines, each of which carries from 160 to 224 nuclear warheads. One alone could destroy the heart of every major Soviet city. Each commander of a Trident II submarine will be able to destroy 408 cities. The navy wants 30 of them by 1990.

If deterrence of a nuclear attack were the sole object of the nuclear-arms race, all talk about "balance" would be meaningless. That balance was achieved long ago when each had the capacity to destroy the other and is not affected by further additions to "overkill" capacity. Nor do differences in technical characteristics have any significance for national security if the objective is deterrence of a nuclear attack. Thus, for example, there is a race to make missiles more accurate, since the closer one comes to its target the more likely it will be able to destroy the enemy's missiles on the ground. U.S. missiles are more accurate than Soviet missiles. The Soviets, on the other hand, make larger missiles with a greater "throw weight," which means that they can carry larger weapons. According to General George Brown, chairman of the Joint Chiefs, the Soviets have "an advantage of two to one" in throw weight, which they need because Soviet bombs are bigger. The Center for Defense Information in Washington has calculated that in 1974 the Soviets had 718,538 times the destructive power that obliterated Hiroshima. The United States was a poor second, with a stockpile of only 369,769 times the Hiroshima-strength bomb!

As long as the U.S. and Soviet political leaders share a consensus that nuclear war is unthinkable and that nuclear weapons are useful only for creating a prospect of Armageddon, there is no good argument for continuing the arms race. Unfortunately, military planners in the United States and in the Soviet Union have bureaucratic interests in keeping their political superiors from arriving at such a consensus. The U.S. military have long operated on the assumption that nuclear wars can be fought and won, for the simple reason that much of the military establishment and its procurement programs would be superfluous without such an assumption. At

a critical moment in the SALT negotiations, when he was under attack
from the military for his proposals, Henry Kissinger exclaimed, "What, in
the name of God, is strategic superiority? What is the significance of it
politically, militarily, operationally at these levels of numbers? What do
you do with it?" For most of the nuclear age the Pentagon has had an
answer. Counterforce. Simply stated, the strategic plan calls for targeting
Soviet missiles and other military targets, in addition to cities, in order to
keep those missiles from hitting the United States. The assumption behind
such a "damage-limiting" strategy is either that the United States will strike
first, as the U.S. Government indicated that it will do in the case of an
invasion of Europe, or that if the Soviets start a surprise nuclear war, they
will hold back some of their forces for what the Pentagon calls "follow-on
attacks." (If the Soviets launched their whole force at once, the U.S.
counterforce strike would land on empty silos instead of missiles.) From
the Eisenhower administration on, the master war plan, known as SIOP
(Strategic Integrated Operations Plan), has called for targeting both Soviet
cities and weapons. "We have regularly targeted military targets," Secretary Schlesinger declared in 1974. What has changed is the military doctrine, which now assumes the possibility of "controlled" nuclear exchanges
at "intermediate" levels of conflict. Thus, as one Pentagon planner told
me, the United States might destroy a Soviet missile base as a "warning"
to the Kremlin to moderate their provocative behavior, or the Strategic
Air Command might "take out" a city as a demonstration of the President's
will—all without courting Armageddon.

Until recently U.S. strategists assumed that the Soviet Union had a
different strategy. Because they had far fewer weapons, they had nothing
more sophisticated than a doomsday policy. If attacked, they would let
their missiles fly in such way as to wreak maximum havoc in the United
States. In 1976, however, the Department of Defense gave a top secret
briefing to the President purporting to show that if the Soviets launched
an attack, ten times as many Americans would die as Soviet citizens. This
meant, Pentagon argued, that the Kremlin was now actively seeking the
military capacity to fight and "win" a nuclear war by striking first at a
U.S. military target and holding back a retaliatory force to "blackmail"
the United States into submission. Paul Nitze argues that the Soviets are
seeking a "theoretical war-winning capability," because they are improving
the accuracy of their missiles, building larger ones, making a major effort
in civil defense to keep their own casualties down in the event of war, and
are dispersing and hardening their military plants.

The U.S. Air Force is developing a larger, more accurate ICBM, known as Missile X, to replace the present Minuteman system, likely to cost as much as $30 billion. In the hope that it can deny the Soviets a "theoretical war-winning capability," the weapon is designed to fight the limited counterforce war that former Secretary of Defense James Schlesinger said was an essential new element of a sound national security strategy. According to Lieutenant General Alton D. Slay, deputy chief of staff for research and development, it is the only strategic weapon "that has a prompt, high-confidence counterforce capability." The development of the weapon will undermine the SALT agreements, which depend upon satellite reconnaissance for verification. It is now relatively easy to photograph missile silos and determine whether the numerical limits imposed by the treaty are being observed. Missile X will be mobile and will probably operate in a highly complex underground subway system. Since the missiles will be in continuous motion underground, they will be almost impossible for the Soviets to locate and target.

The other new U.S. strategic systems, the cruise missile and the Trident submarine, which will cost at least another $30 billion to develop, are urged as a necessary measure to counter the greater accuracy, increased flexibility, and greater striking power of the new Soviet nuclear force. The Soviet improvements, as one might expect, mirror previous developments in the U.S. force. The explicit assumption behind SALT II was that each side would be free to make such qualitative improvements in its force as long as the numerical limits were observed. But what one side sees as "moderation" the other is likely to see as a deadly threat. The qualitative arms race is more destabilizing than the quantitative race because it can be read as a sophisticated indicator of the intentions of the adversary.

The most controversial evidence that the Soviet Union is seeking a "theoretical war-winning capability" under the cloak of détente concerns civil defense. Lord Chalfont, former defense correspondent for the London *Times* and minister of state in the British cabinet, thinks, along with Paul Nitze, "that the nuclear balance, always a fragile and uncertain edifice, is being demolished before our very eyes," because the Soviet Union "is resolved to acquire the capacity in the very near future . . . to deliver an effective nuclear attack and survive the ensuing retaliation." The case for asserting that the Soviets are seeking a "first strike" capability rests a good deal on their civil defense program. The Soviets spend more on shelters, manuals, and drills than the United States—about $65 billion in the last decade, compared with $17 billion in the United States. The program is considered important by some Pentagon officials because it is headed by a Colonel General Altunin, a member of the Soviet Central Committee, and employs perhaps as many as 100,000 people. With such a program, Nitze argues, the Soviets could count on losing "only" 10 to 20 million people in a well-executed surprise attack on the United States.

"Congress is about to be stampeded by a 'civil defense gap,' " Congressman Les Aspin, a former Pentagon analyst, warns. It will turn out, he suggests, to be as exaggerated as the bomber gaps and missile gaps of earlier years. (In the bizarre world of nuclear strategy, satire is impossible. The culmination of *Dr. Strangelove,* a 1964 movie spoofing the nuclear-arms race, is a hysterical warning about the "mine-shaft gap," which will allow the Soviet Union to save more of its population in a nuclear war than the United States. Eight years later Pentagon officials had a briefing on the mine-shaft gap for congressional committees.) Much of the evidence for the extensive and efficient Soviet civil defense program comes from unclassified Soviet manuals that describe a vast shelter program, evacuation exercises, and other forms of civil defense. But, as Aspin argues, the "rumblings of bureaucrats don't amount to effective protection." You can find U.S. manuals that also give a euphoric picture of the "post-attack environment." (Indeed, many of the Soviet manuals turn out to be translations of U.S. manuals.) At the height of the last bomb-shelter scare in 1961, Edward Teller, one of our distinguished scientists, wrote an article in *Life* magazine making the absurd claim that "99% could be saved." I recall a manual from the United States Employment Service from that era entitled, if I remember correctly, "How to Find a Job in the Post-Attack Environment." On the cover was a friendly bureaucrat behind a desk. The applicant was filling out a form. In the background a mushroom cloud was just beginning to disperse.

In reality the Soviet Union has as great a problem saving its population in a nuclear war as the United States, and perhaps a greater one. In both countries about 40 percent of the population is concentrated in ten cities, but the area of the Soviet cities is about half that of the U.S. cities and makes an easier target. Thus while the Soviet Government has been trying to disperse its population and industry since the 1930s for economic and political reasons, its population is actually more concentrated than that of the United States. A fallout-shelter program must be able to protect the population not just for a few hours but for thirty days or more. In the early 1960s the U.S. Office of Civil Defense calculated that it would take up to 20 percent of the adult population of the United States to run a program of that magnitude. There is no evidence that a program on such a scale exists in the Soviet Union. Moreover, to reduce casualties to what U.S. strategists call "acceptable limits," large segments of the population would have to be evacuated. The Soviets have plans, it appears, to evacuate the top leaders, just the way the United States does. (Perhaps the best way to tell how important one is in the Washington hierarchy is whether one has been issued a reservation card for a berth in the secret command center in the Maryland mountains to which the top leadership will repair in the event of a nuclear war.) But neither country has the capability to evacuate millions, the Soviets even less of one because of their severe climate. As the top civil defense official of the Carter administration has testified, the alarmism about Soviet civil defense is unfounded. The fact that the Soviets abandoned the ABM is probably the best evidence that they have given up any hope of avoiding devastating casualties in a nuclear war.

I once had the grisly assignment in the Department of Defense of working on one of the periodic estimates the military like to make about how many will die in the event various "nuclear options" are employed. So many unverifiable assumptions about the nature of the attack, weather conditions, the secondary effects of a monumental disaster—fallout, disease, panic—are implicit in such estimates that no one, except perhaps the statisticians of death who prepare them, has any confidence in them. Ultimately the barrage of facts and figures nuclear strategists hurl at political leaders can be reduced to a single psychological question: Would a rational Soviet political leader begin a war if he believed that an unpredictable number of Soviet citizens, but a minimum of 20 million or more, would surely die? If the question is answered in the negative, there is no justification whatever for the projected "improvements" and additions to the U.S. nuclear arsenal. If the answer is "yes" or even "maybe," there is no escape from a permanent escalating arms race and a high probability of nuclear war. If, indeed, Soviet leaders are bent on creating the impression that they think they can win a nuclear war, improving the U.S. missile force will not help, since the Soviets, if they care enough, can match each improvement with an improvement of their own. It matters little how effective the improvements are. Lasers, ray guns, "killer satellites," fascinate military technologists who, on both sides, have a professional interest in the nostalgic illusion of victory through secret weapons. That illusion is the essence of the arms race mentality which still pervades U.S. and Soviet strategy.

Because these old attitudes now persist against a backdrop of nuclear proliferation—thirty-five nations, the Swedish Institute of Peace Research estimates, will be able to make nuclear bombs within nine years—veteran arms analysts, including George Rathjens of M.I.T. and Thomas Schelling of Harvard, have written that nuclear war is inevitable by the year 2000. The professional and popular perceptions in the era of détente are almost exactly the reverse of what they were fifteen years ago. Then the experts dismissed popular fears about radioactivity, spread of nuclear weapons, nuclear accident, and the "simplistic notion" that arms races inevitably lead to war while thousands marched to "ban the bomb." Now the experts write alarmist articles in professional journals and the streets are silent.

Until the détente era no one talked about a U.S.-Soviet naval arms race. The U.S. Navy was supreme. There was virtually no bit of water in the world beyond the reach of a U.S. armada. The Soviet Union was largely landlocked; most of its ports were frozen much of the year. Czarist Russia had never been a sea power. It was highly improbable that Soviet Russia would become one. Within the last five years, however, the mood has shifted dramatically. Admiral Elmo Zumwalt, former chief of naval operations, who, according to skeptical colleagues, modernized the navy by sinking more American ships than any foreign admiral ever did, ran unsuccessfully for the Senate in Virginia on the issue of a composite missile gap and vessel gap. High administration officials have warned of increasing Soviet military activity, particularly in the Indian Ocean, and have argued that the current and projected building programs in the Soviet Union will "upset the naval balance."

There is no question that there has been a Soviet naval buildup. The controversial issues have to do with its extent and significance. As in the nuclear-arms race, numbers can be used to create wildly different pictures of the world. Advocates of a bigger U.S. Navy talk in alarmist terms about the fact that the Soviets have more ships today than the United States. But most of them are small and designed for coastal defense. The U.S. Navy is made up of far larger and more powerful ships and, unlike the Soviet Navy, is designed to project its power on a global scale. Admiral Julien J. LeBourgeois, president of the Naval War College, concludes that it is impossible to "demonstrate conclusively that the Soviet Union has opted for a maritime capability which could support the establishment and defense of distant sea lanes of communication and overseas projection of power against significant opposition."

The evidence that the Soviet Union is trying to become a global naval power is easy to state and hard to evaluate. At the end of the World War II the Soviet Navy was a coastal defense force—in effect, a branch of the army. Gradually, in the fifties, the Soviets built nuclear submarines and ships to oppose U.S. carriers. Recently they have begun to build the Kiev-class aircraft carrier, which, in Admiral LeBourgeois's words, "will provide some air power projection capability beyond Soviet vital land and sea areas." In the 1960s, Soviet ships began to appear in places they had never been before, principally the eastern Mediterranean and the Indian Ocean. By the 1970s they had acquired an overseas base at the port of Berbera in Somalia, had tried to establish a submarine fueling facility at Cienfuegos, Cuba—but backed off under American pressure—and had substantially increased their port calls in many parts of the world. In the Middle East war of 1973, Soviet naval deployments in the Mediterranean, which has been an American lake for a generation, were bolder than in the past. There was a Soviet naval presence off Angola at the height of the 1976 war.

What, then, does this add up to? Both alarmists who warn that the United States is about to slip from its position as number one naval power and those who are more impressed with the propaganda power of the U.S. Navy than the fire power of the Soviet Navy agree that as of today the Soviet Union has a strongly defense-oriented naval strategy. Since the United States presumably has no intention of attacking the Soviet Union, a powerful defense force poses no threat to the United States. Admiral Gene LaRocque, director of the Center for Defense Information in Washington, D.C., puts it this way:

> Unlike the Royal Navy in the 18th and 19th centuries or the American Navy in the 20th century, the Soviet fleet is not designed to fight a sustained offensive naval war far from home. Moscow's naval strategy can best be characterized as "sea denial" rather than "sea control." In practical terms, this means that the Soviet Navy's basic mission is to prevent America or other Western states from using the seas to launch a nuclear attack and as avenues for moving war supplies, and to prevent American forces from conducting amphibious operations . . . Clearly, the Soviet Navy is designed for a short-term war close to the homeland.

Whether the prospects for naval confrontation between the United States and the Soviet Union will increase depends not only upon what new vessels the Soviets build but on what expanded meaning they may now give to "defense." The United States has taken the position for more than a generation that a worldwide string of bases and far-flung naval operations were essential to the "defense of the Free World." It appears that, as with respect to nuclear weapons, Soviet naval theory and practice is increasingly imitative of the U.S. example. The construction of aircraft carriers is explicitly designed to deny the United States the complete freedom to undertake distant military operations that the Pentagon has had in the past. "During the recent Angola episode," Admiral LeBourgeois writes, "Soviet naval forces were positioned to lend moral and military support to the MPLA and to protect the ships and aircraft carrying materials to Angola." The forces were there to symbolize the Soviet commitment and to dramatize the risks of a larger U.S. intervention. Soviet strategists argue that it is as legitimate for the Soviet Union to protect its clients with naval forces far from its territory as for the United States. Indeed, having the option to send flotillas to "trouble spots" is a hallmark of a great power. The Soviet Union is making an implicit claim that parity means being able to match the United States in its military behavior in the Third World, but at this point there is nothing to suggest that the Kremlin is prepared to make the huge investment necessary to press that claim.

Admiral Elmo Zumwalt was a virtuoso campaigner for big navy budgets. "There has been a dramatic change in the maritime balance between ourselves and the Soviet Union . . . We stand now at our point of greatest weakness and in my estimate our greatest jeopardy." Former Secretary Schlesinger once called such views "alarmist," and Senator John Stennis, of the Armed Services Committee, wrote an essay in 1974 criticizing those who "have something to sell" for having "oversold the strength of our possible adversaries and . . . undersold our own strength." Nonetheless the navy in recent years has dramatically increased its budget and now receives the largest share of the total. The 1976 budget calls for a 16 percent increase in the navy's share over the previous year. Zumwalt's successor has been more moderate in his rhetoric, although not in his budget requests. The crucial question, says Admiral Holloway, is "not which navy is 'number one' " but "whether the U.S. Navy can adequately carry out its missions and tasks in support of our national strategy." For the foreseeable future, he reported to Congress in 1975, the U.S. Navy can successfully carry out its mission against Soviet threat.

In the era of détente the mission of the U.S. Navy has been expanding. It continues to prepare for nuclear war and to guard the commercial sea lanes. Since the oil boycott of 1973 the latter function has been stressed at budget time. Even a year earlier the secretary of the navy told the

National Security Industrial Association that increasing U.S. dependence on imported raw materials required an expanded navy.

> While we occupy only 6% of the total land mass of the earth, we consume nearly 30% of all energy produced on an annual basis. It is estimated that by 1985 we will have to import one-half of our petroleum needs—something on the order of 12 million barrels of crude oil per day . . . and will require a Navy capable of assuring their safe passage. It will require a Navy capable of seeing that oil-producing countries are not subjected to such pressures that the flow subsides.
>
>   But oil is not our only import. You are aware that 69 of 72 vital raw materials, without which our business could not function, are wholly or in part imported into the United States.

Pentagon strategists argue that the United States needs a much larger navy than the Soviet Union because we are, as Henry Kissinger has put it, an "island power" in the tradition of the British Empire, dependent on the sea for access to energy sources, vital metals for the industrial system, and markets. The Soviet Union, on the other hand, though lacking warm-water ports and the open sea, produces most of the energy sources and minerals it needs from the huge land mass under its direct control. If the Soviet Union were in a position to restrict U.S. access to raw materials, that would indeed represent a shift in the balance of power. At this point, however, not even the most alarmist admirals argue that the Soviet Union is seeking such a capability or could acquire it if it wanted to, given the huge preponderance of U.S. naval power.

The most dramatic expansion in the mission of the U.S. Navy is something the Pentagon calls "naval presence" and "power projection." These are modern terms for what used to be called "gunboat diplomacy." Admiral Stansfield Turner, now head of the C.I.A., defines "naval presence" as "the use of naval forces, short of war, to achieve political objectives." This is done by dispatching ships to potential crisis areas to warn potential enemies or to reassure friends. When an aircraft carrier or a destroyer with nuclear weapons takes up a position offshore or calls at port, it is an immediate and tangible expression of American military might. "To the citizen of a less technologically oriented society," says Admiral Zumwalt, "nothing is quite like a shipshape destroyer making a call." Gunboat diplomacy has been a standard mission of the U.S. Navy since its founding, but its role increased in the Nixon-Kissinger years. The United States can no longer field a land army in Asia, and probably not in Latin America or Africa either, because the domestic political consensus for "another Vietnam" is lacking. The navy, in Admiral Zumwalt's words, is a "high technology, capital intensive" service which does not demand the involvement of sufficient numbers of young Americans to cause political trouble.

The dispatch of a naval force can have a powerful psychological impact abroad and cause little stir at home. Thus, during the Syrian attack on Jordan in September 1970, two U.S. aircraft carriers were moved off the Israeli coast to lend credence to a U.S. diplomatic effort to persuade Syria to withdraw. A year later, when Indian troops invaded what is now Bangladesh, the United States ordered a naval task force, led by the aircraft carrier *Enterprise,* into the Bay of Bengal. It was a symbolic show of support for the Pakistanis. More important, it established the "routine practice" of U.S. vessels operating in the Indian Ocean. In 1974 the navy began similar "routine" operations in the Persian Gulf. When Israeli commandos freed passengers of an airplane held hostage by Palestinian hijackers at Entebbe, in Uganda, on July 11, 1976, and Uganda President Idi Amin threatened retaliation against Kenya for helping the rescue operation, the United States promptly sent a frigate to Kenya for a "courtesy port call" and dispatched the aircraft carrier *Ranger* to the Indian Ocean for "routine periodic deployment." Privately the U.S. officials made it clear that these were expressions of support for Kenya designed to "stabilize" the situation.

There have been, according to a Brookings Institution study, some 215 such incidents between 1945 and 1975 in which the United States has used military force as a political instrument. In about 85 percent of the cases, the navy was used to make the point. (In the same period, according to the Brookings study, the Soviets carried out a similar show of force on 70 occasions.) The appearance of warships can convey a variety of threats— from harassment to blockade to air strikes. James Schlesinger once suggested that recalcitrant Third World nations could be punished for policies hostile to the United States through some form of blockade. There would be protests, but "the long run therapeutic effect on other states of such action might be substantial."

In the détente years political tensions in Europe have subsided, but the military buildup on the Continent has continued. The confrontation between NATO forces and the Warsaw Pact armies constitutes the third arms race between the United States and the Soviet Union. Like the nuclear-arms race, the "conventional arms balance in Europe" has been the subject of lengthy and complex negotiations, the so-called Mutual and Balanced Force Reductions talks, which began on October 20, 1973, in Vienna. The talks have generated several tons of paper and some long-term leases in the Vienna suburbs, but nothing else.

The agreements between the Federal Republic of Germany and the Soviet Union and the quadripartite agreements on Berlin, which recognized East Germany and the continued access rights of the West in Berlin, removed the issues over which the United States and the Soviet Union had come close to war on several occasions. The agreements were, therefore, a crucial step in defusing the confrontation between the nuclear powers. But they have led to an arms buildup rather than an arms reduction. Since the end of the Vietnam War the United States has added three army divisions and four air force wings which have been primarily designated for the defense of Europe. The Soviet Union is modernizing and expanding its forces in central Europe. As Secretary of Defense Schlesinger announced in 1975, "most of our forces already are or soon will be oriented toward a war in Europe." There are about 300,000 U.S. military personnel in Europe organized in five divisions, two armored cavalry regiments and 22 tactical fighter squadrons. The United States also maintains an airlift capability to fly in an additional two and one half divisions from the United States within days. There are more than 7,000 U.S. tactical nuclear weapons in Europe. The whole structure of the U.S. Army, according to Chief of Staff Frederick C. Weyand, is "pretty much keyed to NATO." For the air force "the NATO scenario is the dominant factor in determining the level and capabilities of our tactical forces." All this costs about $35 billion a year, the Center for Defense Information calculates, although the budget is not written in a way to permit one to find out easily how much money goes for the NATO commitment. (When the United States had almost 600,000 troops in Vietnam in 1969, the annual cost was $21.5 billion.)

Because of the expense and the obvious reluctance of the European countries themselves to bear a greater part of it, a minority in Congress, led for many years by former Senate Majority Leader Mike Mansfield, has tried unsuccessfully to cut the U.S. military presence in Europe. General T. R. Milton, the first chairman of the NATO working group on Mutual and Balanced Force Reductions, says that "the work was begun in NATO with one principal objective: the pacification of Senator Mansfield." U.S. policy remains what it was in 1972 when President Nixon declared, "The policy of this government is to maintain and improve our forces in Euope and not reduce them except through reciprocal reductions negotiated with the Warsaw Pact." The MBFR talks have been stalled from the start because, as Schlesinger has said, "the conceptual bases of the Eastern and Western proposals are fundamentally different." The NATO proposals start from the premise that the West is in an inferior position militarily. Therefore, to reach the agreed ceilings of 700,000 men each for NATO and Warsaw Pact forces in central Europe, the Soviets should withdraw more. The Soviets argue that the present situation is "stable" and hence the cuts should be an equal percentage for both sides. The United States has also proposed exchanging a reduction of 1,000 tactical nuclear weapons for a cut of 1,700 in Soviet tanks. Neither side takes the proposals of the other side seriously.

The SALT talks, despite the little they have accomplished, reflect the genuine concern of the American and Soviet elites about the dangers of an unbridled nuclear-arms race. No such concern exists in the Vienna talks. The expectation of war is low. The troops on both sides serve a variety of political purposes that leaders in the United States, West Europe, and the Soviet Union are reluctant to abandon. The troops have been facing each other at the Elbe for twenty-five years. No one expects an attack in either direction, but there is considerable nervousness in both alliances at what might happen if the troops should leave.

The European security has been a frozen issue because the real reasons the two armies face each other cannot be candidly stated. General Andrew Goodpaster, former Supreme Allied Commander in Europe, writing twenty years after U.S. divisions were first assigned to NATO, recalls that the question at NATO's birth was not "Will there be a war?" but rather "In what month will war start?" An exhausted Western Europe, "weakened and weary of war, faced a new threat—and it seemed only a matter of time until the threat would be carried out. That was the climate—the harsh, numbing, almost paralyzing climate—into which NATO was born." For almost thirty years the official assumption within the U.S. military has been that the Soviets intended to invade Western Europe and it was only the American commitment to defend it by dropping the bomb on the Soviet Union—a commitment symbolized by a permanent presence of American troops on the Continent—that kept thousands of Soviet tanks from sweeping to the English Channel. That was the myth under which training exercises were conducted, briefings prepared, and hundreds of secret cables exchanged. But it had little basis in fact. If Western Europe was weakened and weary of war in the late 1940s and early 1950s, the

Soviet Union was even more so. With 20 million dead, her industrial base destroyed, lacking adequate rail or road communication to move a great army across Poland, the Soviet Union did not intend to start a general war. We know now, and President Truman and his top advisers believed then, that Stalin's postwar demobilization was so precipitate that a Soviet blitzkrieg was quite out of the question.

Despite the alarmist predictions of generals in the field—in March 1948 Lucius Clay, the American Commander in Germany, sent an "eyes only" cable to the President describing his "feeling" that war "may come with dramatic suddenness"—the official view of the Soviet threat at the highest levels of the Truman administration was far more moderate. The Soviets, as George Kennan, the leading State Department Russian expert, put it at the time, had no "grand design" and did not intend, in particular, to pursue their competition with us by means of a general war. President Truman, Kennan wrote in his diary in 1952, "shared my views as to the motives and principles of behavior of the Soviet leaders, and had never believed that they wanted another great war." Three years earlier John Foster Dulles, who was a senator from New York when the North Atlantic Treaty was being debated, after being briefed by Secretary of State Acheson and others, concluded that "the information given me, publicly and privately, by our own government and by heads and leaders of European governments, does not indicate that the Soviet Union now contemplates large-scale military aggression in Europe." This was also the repeated view of James Forrestal during the early postwar years when he was secretary of defense.

The original purpose of NATO was to build up military strength in West Europe as a "modest shield," to use Kennan's words, behind which the governments of West Europe could overcome what Dean Acheson called their "widespread sense of insecurity." The insecurity stemmed not from fear of imminent attack by the Russian hordes but from economic paralysis, the political strength of local communist parties under the control of Moscow—there were communists in the cabinet in Italy and France as late as May 1947—and the lack of a compelling noncommunist ideology. The original emphasis of the European Recovery Program was economic; the military commitments were to create the confidence to make economic recovery possible. Originally NATO was a guarantee pact, not an international army at permanent battle stations. "None of us dreamed at the time," Kennan recalls, "that the constructive impulses of this enterprise would be overtaken and swallowed up in the space of a mere two or three years by programs of military assistance based on a wholly different concept of the Soviet threat and of Europe's needs." After the Korean invasion of 1950 Dean Acheson called for the creation of a German army within NATO. His justification was that "the international communist movement has shown that it does not hesitate to use force to conquer a sovereign and independent state." But his reasons for pressing German rearmament, which he had recommended before the Korean invasion, had less to do with the Soviet threat—U.S. intelligence concluded that Korea was a "local affair" and did not foreshadow an attack in Europe—than with the shape of European politics. The postwar generation of American planners lived with the nightmare that Germany might be sucked into the Soviet orbit, because the Kremlin by its control of East Germany held the key to reunification. To prevent this possibility, West Germany would be tightly integrated into a community of West European nations tied economically and militarily to the United States. The presence of five U.S. divisions on German soil would restrict West Germany's room for political maneuver. Once Europe recovered and became less dependent upon the United States economically, the military alliance would continue to serve as political glue.

None of this could be conveniently explained to the public. The early cold-war period was not a time for subtlety, but rather, in Acheson's words, for bludgeoning "the mass mind of 'top government' " and "preaching" to the public. "Qualification must give way to simplicity of statement, nicety and nuance to bluntness, almost brutality in carrying home a point . . . If we did make our points clearer than truth, we did not differ from most other educators and could hardly do otherwise." But images created for momentary political effect persist long after the subtle policies they mask have been forgotten. It has been almost twenty years since the dramatic economic recovery of West Europe. The major communist parties of the region are no longer under the domination of Moscow. The issue of German reunification, if not settled, has receded into the background. Yet the array of military force in the heart of Europe is more imposing than ever.

Why is it so difficult to negotiate an agreement for "balanced and mutual" force reductions? One reason is that it is almost impossible to agree on what "balance" means. Both alliances have roughly the same number of troops in the field—about 1.7 million. NATO has approximately 9,000 tanks in central Europe, the Warsaw Pact has about 15,500 (with perhaps another 25,000 in reserve). U.S. tanks, according to the

Pentagon, are better. The United States and its allies outnumber the Soviets in antitank weapons, and they are technologically superior to their Soviet counterparts. The NATO air forces, according to Air Force Chief of Staff General Jones, "are a far more potent combat force" than the Warsaw Pact air force. These factors tend to offset the Soviet advantage in tanks, but how much no one can say for sure in advance of an actual combat. The Soviets are supposed to have an enormous geographical advantage because they can reinforce their troops from Russia, only 1,500 miles away, while the U.S. supply lines are 3,500 miles long. But former Secretary of Defense Schlesinger has testified that "with our airlift capabilities, we are able to redeploy combat troops very quickly, in fact more quickly in a number of respects than the Soviets can in a location closer at hand." The U.S. military take a professionally conservative view of all these factors and continually call for improvements in military equipment. The Soviets, too, aware that some U.S. officers disparage their tank force and World War II tactics for using them as obsolete, are rapidly modernizing their force. The process of modernization, however normal and reasonable it may appear to one side, looks threatening to the other. The Soviets have also increased their troops in East Germany to match the rapid growth of the West German Army, which has been given responsibility for defending about 50 percent of the front. Even in the mid-1960s, James Schlesinger had observed, "German forces possessed limited capabilities." They can now put 1.2 million men in the field on short notice and have thus "grown to be a very formidable deterrent." To the Soviets the German forces are not a deterrent but a potential invasion force. In the MBFR talks they have pressed for a reduction of the German troops, but the United States has opposed such efforts. NATO has become a U.S.-German military alliance, the nightmare that Stalin and his successors tried so ineptly to prevent.

But the most important reasons why neither side is interested in tampering with the military arrangements in Europe are political. For the Soviet Union the troops serve a police function. The only occasions on which Warsaw Pact troops have been used in battle have been invasions of two members—Hungary in 1956 and Czechoslovakia in 1968. The Kremlin is determined, as Brezhnev made clear after the overthrow of Dubcek, that the heresies now sweeping what used to be called "world communism" will not be permitted to challenge Soviet domination of East Europe. As the legitimacy of Soviet hegemony weakens, the role of military force becomes ever more important. The United States, having abandoned the illusions of "rollback" and "liberation" dispensed so freely in John Foster Dulles' day, sees the Soviet troops in East Europe as a guarantor of stability. No one in the upper reaches of the State Department likes to imagine what would happen if the troops pulled out. There would be rapid political change and in all likelihood a severe Soviet reaction. The "organic" relationship between East Europe and the Soviet Union recommended in Helmut Sonnenfeldt's indiscreetly worded memorandum to U.S. ambassadors—which became a minor campaign issue in 1976—is preferred to the dangers and uncertainties of a process of liberation.

The official U.S. perception of the Soviet threat in Europe today is much like the perception of the nuclear threat. It is hard to find a general in the Pentagon who thinks it any more likely that the Soviets will invade Germany than that they will launch a nuclear war. Why the Soviets would want to do either is mysterious, for victory would offer as many disasters as defeat. Soviet control of East Europe is tenuous; prolonged occupation of West Europe would hardly be a stable basis for expanding Soviet power. Attempting to dominate the world economy after a nuclear war in which the U.S. economy is destroyed cannot be an attractive fantasy for rational leaders, however cunning, who are painfully aware that they cannot even manage the Soviet economy.

What generals now say they worry about is the development of "war-fighting capabilities." If the Soviets acquire the look of a superior military power, they will be able to translate the fear that this will inspire among the West Europeans into political concessions. This is the so-called "Finlandization" thesis. West Europe, like Finland, will tailor its foreign policies to suit the Soviet Union because of the preponderance of military power on its borders. The Finns, to be sure, make compromises to keep Soviet troops out of their country. They do not print Solzhenitsyn, but they import copies in Finnish from Sweden. The Finns resent the notion that their internal politics are dominated by the Soviet Union, because they have preserved parliamentary democracy and they do not follow any variant of the Soviet model.

The "Finlandization" slogan appears to be a code word for a distinctly different set of fears in Western Europe. In France, Germany, Italy, and the Low Countries anticommunism has been a powerful conservative force in domestic politics. The Soviet threat has been a rallying point for organizing domestic anticommunist coalitions. In the détente years two seemingly contradictory trends have changed European perceptions. The U.S.-Soviet rapprochement, and the agreements on Berlin and Germany in particular, reduced the tension in Europe and rendered the military threat from the Soviets even less credible than it had been before. At the same time the decline in U.S. prestige as a consequence of the Vietnam disaster engendered the feeling that a long-term balance of power unfavorable to the West was in process. Particularly because of Kissinger's shock-style diplomacy, the fear of a U.S.-Soviet deal on Europe grew.

But the alternative to the Atlanticist vision of the 1950s, a Gaullist Europe from the Pyrenees to the Urals, seems more remote than ever. There is no strong European leader. France has dropped its anti-American posture, but its power has been dwarfed by Germany's. The consequence of the new relationship between America and Russia is that the Soviet threat is no longer strong enough glue to bind nations that, increasingly, have come to see themselves as having divergent interests. Outside of Portugal there is no strong party, even those calling themselves communist, that is pro-Soviet. Ironically, some of NATO's most vocal boosters are the Italian communists, the very group that the alliance was supposed to keep from ever coming to power.

CHAPTER 6
The Business of Peace

From Henry Wallace to Henry Kissinger, theorists of détente have believed that the logic of economics can temper the irrationality of politics. Wallace, like Kissinger, believed that American policy should aim at providing the Soviets an economic stake in maintaining world peace. "We know that much of the recent Soviet behavior that has caused us concern," Wallace, then secretary of commerce, wrote President Truman on March 15, 1946, "has been the result of their dire economic needs and of their disturbed sense of security." Like 90 percent of the businessmen who responded to a *Fortune* poll in September 1945, Wallace believed it was in U.S. interest to promote trade with Russia. Bringing the Soviet Union out of economic isolation would relieve their anxieties and force them to be responsible citizens. Long before "linkage" became a Kissinger code word for using economic bait to influence political behavior, the idea struck American businessmen as common sense.

Donald Kendall, once a vocal anticommunist, now serves as cochairman of the American-Soviet Trade and Economic Council, an official organization established by intergovernment agreement to promote economic relations. He has been an indefatigable lobbyist for closer U.S.-Soviet economic ties. "I think trade is going to be one of the main means of solving the problems between the United States and the Soviet Union." It all started twenty years ago when he accompanied Richard Nixon to the "kitchen debate" with Khrushchev. (In the famous 1958 photograph a subdued Brezhnev is shown, off at the side, holding a Pepsi.) By the time of his next visit to Russia, Nixon had acquired Pepsi as a principal client and spent part of his time trying to get the soft drink into the Soviet market. The Kendall-Nixon connection impressed the Soviets, and one of the most publicized deals in the era of détente was a barter arrangement in which Pepsi would be bottled for sale in the Soviet Union and Kendall's company would import Stolichnaya vodka into the United States. Linkage, Kendall believes, has worked. "In Chile you had an elected government that was elected communist, and I think that anybody who knows the power of the Soviet Union knows that, if they wanted to maintain that government in Chile, that Allende would still be there today. But I think this is a sign of change in their policy that did not occur at the time of Cuba, and you know the results of that."

Whether increased economic relations with the Soviet Union had anything to do with their failure to respond to the U.S. destabilization campaign in Chile is dubious. At a time when the United States had minimal economic relations with Russia it conducted a successful coup against the elected government of Guatemala in 1954, invaded the Dominican Republic in 1965, and pursued an active anticommunist policy throughout the hemisphere without evoking a Soviet response. The linkage between politics and economics is much more subtle than détente enthusiasts from the business world like to picture it.

In the cold-war years U.S. policy toward Russia was predicated on a different sort of linkage. Instead of using credits, technology, and long-term economic relationships as incentives for good political behavior, successive administrations tried withholding them as a way of forcing the Soviets into cooperation on American terms. Lend-lease aid was summarily stopped at the end of the war, and the Soviet request for a $1 billion loan in 1946 was ignored. True, after internal debate in the State Department the Russians were invited to participate in the Marshall Plan for the recovery of Europe in 1947, but the terms were such as to make it inevitable that Stalin would decline. The United States, not wishing to subsidize the consolidation of Soviet power in Eastern Europe, insisted on controlling how the money was to be spent. But the last thing Stalin was prepared to accept was the assertion of American political influence in his newly acquired empire, and the Soviets withdrew from the Marshall Plan, forcing Czechoslovakia to go with them. Thereafter the United States mounted a campaign of economic warfare against the Soviet Union as a centerpiece of its containment policy. Under the Export Control Act of 1949 nothing of potential military or strategic value could be exported to the Soviet Union and other communist countries unless the exporter acquired a special license from the Department of Commerce. At the height of the cold war there were over 1,000 proscribed items, including almost anything that the Soviets might wish to import. "Everything has a potential military significance," Bernard Baruch used to say, "except, possibly, bubble gum." In 1962 the act was toughened to prohibit the export of goods of any "economic significance." The United States hoped that an economic boycott could change Soviet policy or weaken Soviet power.

A further measure to increase economic pressure on the Soviet Union by barring private credit was the Johnson Act, originally passed in 1934 to prohibit American citizens and corporations from lending money to any country that had not paid its war debt to the United States. After the Second World War the act was amended to permit loans to countries that were part of the Western economic system by virtue of membership in the World Bank and the International Monetary Fund. Since the Soviets had paid neither the prerevolutionary debt nor the lend-lease debt, this had the effect of keeping the ban in effect only for the communist countries, the Soviet bloc had refused to join these U.S.-dominated capitalist agencies. In 1951 Congress withdrew most-favored-nation treatment from the Soviet Union, a status it had enjoyed since 1935. The importation of Soviet crab meat was banned from 1951 to 1961 under a law prohibiting importation of goods made by convict or forced labor. A flat ban on importing Soviet or Communist Chinese ermine, mink, muskrat, and weasel continues to this day. The United States during these years used its power over the economies of West Europe to induce their cooperation in enforcing economic isolation of the Soviet Union.

What was the effect of these policies on Soviet behavior? For one thing, they helped to reinforce and in a sense legitimize Stalin's view of the world economy. The Soviet dictator in the 1930s virtually closed the Soviet economy to foreign trade. In 1937, exports and imports each amounted to only one half of 1 percent of the gross national product, compared with 10 to 12 percent before the revolution. Stalin argued the goal of national self-sufficiency, and Soviet economists who remained in favor said that autarchy, freedom from the necessity to trade, was the objective of Soviet economic planning. After the war the Soviet trading bloc was expanded to include Eastern Europe and China, but there was little trading outside the bloc. In Stalin's view the world was divided into "two camps," each with its own self-contained economic system. It is unlikely that a more liberal trading policy in the West would have cracked Stalin's "closed society," the prime ideological target of the American national security elite, but the belligerent economic policy of the West certainly helped to keep it sealed.

Did the Soviet Union suffer as a result? It is a matter of controversy. The Soviets forced the East European countries to buy their raw materials at artificially high prices. Trade officials in Bulgaria in 1949 and in Czechoslovakia in 1952 were executed for "anti-Soviet and nationalist" behavior because they objected to the terms the Soviets imposed. At the same time, the export prices from the Soviet Union's reluctant trading partners were set too low. There is no doubt that Soviet economic relations with the other communist countries were exploitive in the Stalin years, but by the mid-1960s Soviet economists were complaining that the Soviet Union was supplying valuable raw materials to its East European allies which it needed for its own development, and making itself a dumping ground for manufactured goods from Eastern Europe. In short, the isolation of the Soviet bloc from the rest of the world economy exacerbated the political tensions between the Soviet Union and the East European countries and caused distortions within the Soviet economy. The unavailability of foreign high technology meant that the development of a domestic military industry became a priority, particularly the aircraft and turbine industries. The lack of hard currency for imports of consumer goods, and the low priority assigned to domestic production of cars, refrigerators, and television sets, meant that Soviet citizens had to do without them, and that became a serious political problem for the Soviet leadership, and remains one.

But the U.S.-orchestrated boycott did not stop economic growth. Indeed, the years in which economic warfare was most zealously pursued were the years of the most impressive growth spurts in the U.S.S.R.

By the early fifties the Soviets had rebuilt their shattered economy to its prewar levels. Thereafter the growth rates fell sharply, and productivity is continuing to decline. Marshall I. Goldman, professor of economics at Wellesley College and a specialist on the Soviet economy, believes that the boycott did contribute to the slowdown of Soviet growth, particularly in cutting off access to technology. As Goldman points out, when the restrictions on technology were eased in the détente years, the Soviets bought the very same items they had purchased forty years ago. Thus in 1973 they purchased a set of heat-treating furnaces from the Holcroft Company for the immense Kama River truck-plant project which was almost identical to what they bought for the Gorky automobile plant in the 1930s. In 1974 they purchased two ammonia plants from the Chemical Construction Company similar to what they had purchased from the same company in

1932. "The Soviet Union's failure to duplicate such technology in the interim," says Goldman, "meant that for 40 years the Soviet economy was denied the products that this technology could have provided."

The economic relations between the United States and the Soviet Union have always been overshadowed by the political relations. Trade is a barometer of political attitudes. Does it also determine political attitudes? Kissinger's linkage theory is premised on the belief that it does. (Nations that trade together do not like to make too much trouble for one another because political tension tends to interrupt deliveries. Making war is bad for business. Having a stake in a thriving world economy is an incentive to help keep it going.) Leo Szilard—the physicist who held a patent on the triggering device for the atomic bomb, drafted the letter Albert Einstein sent to President Roosevelt which persuaded the President to make the bomb, and spent the rest of his life trying to get rid of nuclear weapons—was probably the inventor of linkage. He met Khrushchev at the United Nations in 1960 and gave him a safety razor. "Every day there is no war, Mr. Chairman, I will send you a blade."

As recently as 1966 the National Association of Manufacturers opposed liberalization of trade with the Soviet Union, but today the assumptions behind the linkage theory have become the pieties of the business world.

From the beginning the synchronization of economics and politics in U.S.-Soviet relations has been less than perfect. Within months in the early 1920s one branch of the U.S. Government was carrying out famine relief in Russia while another was participating in the allied invasion. In the 1920s when successive secretaries of state were calling the Soviet Government "international outlaws," large American firms were helping to establish the foundations of the Soviet economy. The Albert Kahn Company of Detroit, the designer of the Ford Motor Company's River Rouge plant and some of G.M.'s largest factories, helped set up the Gosproektstroi (State Project Construction Trust), the Soviet organization for designing and building plants, and designed a dozen Soviet factories.

The American capitalist with the longest record of dealing with the Soviets is Armand Hammer, who went to the Soviet Union as a young medical school graduate in 1921 to do relief work, met Lenin, and in the chaos of the aftermath of the civil war arranged some unique commercial deals. Lenin gave him the first concession of the Soviet state, the Alpievsky asbestos mine, and permitted him to set up his own pencil factory. Instead of confiscating them as they did most everything else privately owned, Stalin's government paid good value in cash for both the mine and the pencil factory shortly before Hammer left the Soviet Union in 1932. During his long stay he represented forty U.S. companies, including U.S. Rubber, Parker Pen, and Allis-Chalmers, and in the process acquired a fortune (mostly by picking up czarist art treasures) and a mythic status as a friend of Lenin. This he used to good advantage forty years later when he visited the Kremlin and gave his hosts a tour of Lenin's office.

In 1931 the Soviet Union, though still unrecognized by the United States, was importing two-thirds of all U.S. exports of agricultural equipment and power-driven metal-working equipment. The world depression had little effect on Stalin's autarchic economy, and for a brief period when the world capitalist market for U.S. goods collapsed, the Soviets became quite important for the U.S. economy. International Harvester, General Electric, Du Pont, and Ford supplied equipment, technology, and employees for major Soviet plants. (One employee was Walter Reuther, the future head of the United Auto Workers, who worked for a time in the Gorky automobile plant.) In the interwar period the United States became the major noncommunist exporter to the Soviet Union. French and British businessmen and bankers, whose debts the Bolsheviks refused to honor, were unenthusiastic about extending more credit to the Soviets, while the Americans, who had lost comparatively little, were eager to pick up the business.

By 1973, scarcely two years after the Nixon administration had made its first moves to substitute economic incentives for economic warfare as a more effective way to influence Soviet behavior, the United States, because of the huge grain deal, was once again the largest noncommunist exporter to the Soviet Union. Before 1971, U.S. exports to the Soviets seldom hit $100 million a year. In 1976 they reached almost $2.5 billion, but in nonagricultural exports the United States lagged behind West Germany, France and Japan. The improved political climate helped, but the fundamental reason for the expanding web of economic relations between two ideological antagonists and military rivals is the growing realization among capitalists and state socialists alike that neither system can survive in an economically divided world.

As early as 1951 Stalin began to hint that the Soviet Union had outgrown autarchy. He issued an invitation to foreign businessmen to come to a conference on foreign trade in Moscow held in April 1952. The prospect of opening up the Soviet market attracted many Western businessmen, but the conference led to nothing because the U.S. export controls prevented export of the machinery the Soviets wanted, and they had little to sell. Stalin's successors announced a "new course" in the Soviet economy based on greater emphasis on consumer goods, much of which had to be imported. The United States relaxed its export controls somewhat, largely because the West Europeans were circumventing them and the United States had lost its hold over them. Loss of Marshall Plan aid, which was the sanction in the U.S. law to keep allies from trading with the Soviets, was no longer effective since it was coming to an end anyway. As part of his "peace offensive" Khrushchev began calling for vastly expanded trade with the West. He publicly criticized but did not prevent a U.S.-Polish agreement in 1956 under which the Poles bought surplus agricultural products and the U.S. extended a twenty-year credit of $30 million. This was the year of riots in Poland and revolution in Hungary; Soviet economic exploitation of the Eastern bloc was becoming politically hazardous.

At the same time, Khrushchev was coming to realize that his boast to "overtake and surpass" the United States economy was empty without a heavy infusion of advanced technology from the West. As in the military field, where Khrushchev brandished words to make up for a deficiency in missiles, so also in economics. When Khrushchev was taunting American businessmen during his visit to the United States that they would soon be overtaken by the superior Soviet productive system, productivity was actually declining and the growth rate of the Soviet bloc as a whole was falling rather sharply from what it was in the early 1950s. Khrushchev tried to revitalize his sagging chemical industry by purchasing fifty complete chemical plants from British, German, Italian, and French suppliers. As a result of the 1963 crop failure he purchased 10 million tons of grain from Canada and the United States for several hundred million dollars. The Soviet Union had had serious crop failures before, but Stalin was prepared to let millions of people starve rather than advertise the dependent state of Soviet agriculture or sacrifice scarce foreign exchange by buying grain from the West. By the mid 1960s the Stalinist food policy was no longer a political option for Soviet leaders. Ranking State Department officials now believe that grain purchases from the West are a permanent fixture of Soviet policy, because Soviet leaders have made a political decision to upgrade the diet and it is physically and economically impossible to feed the Soviet population adequately without major imports from the grain-exporting nations, all of which are capitalist.

When Khrushchev fell in 1964 his successors began a major reassessment of the Soviet economy. The most dramatic of Khrushchev's "harebrained schemes" for which he was dismissed was the Cuban missile fiasco, but even more important a factor was his erratic and badly managed agriculture policy and his abortive efforts to decentralize the administration of the Soviet economy. While they took stock of the situation, Kosygin and Brezhnev drastically reduced imports of all kinds. Sovietologists predicted a return to Stalinist autarchy. Then in 1966 there was a sudden change. As Marshall Goldman notes, the new Soviet leaders began to realize that the Soviet planning system was not generating innovations or economic growth sufficient even to approach that of the major Western capitalist countries.

> The prevailing policy of autarchy and isolation was only viable on the assumption that Russian industry could keep pace with (or surpass) the technology developed in the rest of the world. This it seemed to be doing, at least until the 1960's. But while Soviet technology had proven itself in basic metallurgy, atomic energy, astronautics, and defense, there were embarrassing deficiencies in electronics, computers, sophisticated forms of assembly line production, and, as before, chemicals. . . . Ironically . . . they discovered that while they had indeed won the industrial race of the 1950's—for more steel and coal production—the race of the 1960's had shifted to newer, more exotic fields of technology. Here the Russians were as far behind as ever.

The Soviet economy is a classic example of uneven development. The technologically sophisticated sectors in which Soviet leaders have concentrated brains and money coexist with unbelievably primitive sectors that are starved for talent and funds. The rate of growth and sophistication in military equipment is evidence enough that the Soviets have the capability to match the best technology in the West. But their resources are thin and they appear to have been concentrated in the military and other priority sectors of the economy. The planning system is clearly not working well. Building construction, for one thing, is shoddy for the most part, and maintenance is so poor that the process of deterioration begins even before the roof is in place. The U.S.S.R. is supposed to have twice as many people working on research and development as the United States. In the *Sputnik* scare of the late 1950s such facts were sufficient to generate large congressional appropriations for the education race—but it turns out that only 12 percent of Soviet research personnel are assigned to industry. (In the United States about 75 percent of the research and development personnel are employed in industry.) In the years when they were trying to avoid dependence on foreign trade the Soviets would try to increase their technological capability by buying prototypes and reproducing such products as Scotch tape, trucks, mining equipment, even Polaroid cameras. But by the mid-1960s it became evident to the Soviet leadership that this wasn't sufficient to provide the technological skills needed for an advanced industrial society. They began once again to buy whole factories. In August 1966 they announced that Fiat would build a $1.5 billion plant to make cars in the Soviet Union, both for domestic use and for export. Ford was their first choice to build the huge Volga River plant, but Henry Ford turned down their offer for fear of adverse public reaction in the United States.

Despite the ideological competition, the United States has always been for the Soviets the model of the modern society. In the détente era Soviet economists have found appropriate quotations from Lenin about revolution being a blend of revolutionary enthusiasm and American know-how. In Stalin's day the Soviets invented an elaborate mythology in which every important invention, from the telephone to the airplane, was the brainchild of a Russian scientist. By the late 1960s the Soviet Union was sufficiently confident about its own technological achievements to accept the idea that the success of Soviet socialism required massive importation of technology from the capitalist West. The Soviet Union had neither the abundance of money nor the talent to duplicate the expensive process of technological development through which the successful capitalist economies of America, Japan, and West Europe had already gone. The Five Year Plan 1976–1980 calls for "wider participation in the international division of labor and raising the role of foreign economic ties in resolving economic tasks and accelerating scientific and technological progress." The plan calls for an increase in the volume of foreign trade 30 to 35 percent and "new forms of mutually advantageous economic, scientific, and technological cooperation, including the realization of joint projects."

Why was the United States, which had been the leader in economic warfare against the Soviet Union, responsive to the Soviet bid for economic cooperation? A number of circumstances combined to change old attitudes. By the late 1960s it was evident that economic warfare had failed principally because the West Europeans would no longer observe the export controls. After the Fiat deal, West European firms flocked to Moscow and some further large orders resulted. Between 1967 and 1969 West German and Japanese sales to the Soviet Union more than doubled, and French and Japanese exports were up about 70 percent. U.S. companies were unhappy that European competitors were taking over a new and potentially vast market. In 1964 the Senate Foreign Relations Committee conducted a survey of businessmen which showed that a majority favored increasing East-West trade, but almost all the respondents wanted to remain anonymous. At the time, companies that were known to trade with the Soviets risked boycotts organized by the Young Americans for Freedom or other anticommunist groups. In 1964 the Johnson administration encouraged Firestone to build a $50 million synthetic-rubber factory in Romania because the State Department thought it would bolster Romania's independence. The Young Americans for Freedom, with the encouragement of Goodyear, which had lost the contract, threatened to rent a small fleet of airplanes to fly over the Indianapolis speedway with banners denouncing Firestone's pact with communism. Firestone canceled the contract. Companies importing gloves from Czechoslovakia would arrange to have them dropped off in the Netherlands long enough for a "Made in Holland" label to be attached. When the Soviets bought American wheat, the International Longshoremen's Association refused to load it until the administration agreed that at least 50 percent of it had to be carried in American ships.

But by the late 1960s the situation began to change. Prominent businessmen spoke out publicly in favor of increased trade with Russia even though the Vietnam War was at its height. Trade with the Soviet Union promised to help some serious U.S. economic problems. It would begin to reverse the negative balance of trade. In 1971, for the first time in almost a century, the United States imported more goods than it exported. But politics still prevailed over economics. In 1970 Henry Ford II announced from the American Embassy in Moscow that he was considering building a plant near Kazan that would produce 150,000 trucks a year. Three weeks later the secretary of defense publicly attacked the idea, noting that the Soviets were supplying trucks to North Vietnam, and the deal was dead. The next year Mack Trucks Inc. was also pressured to drop a contract to supply $750 million worth of truck-manufacturing equipment. Former Nixon administration officials say that these interventions were designed to keep the economic détente from getting ahead of the political détente. In late 1971 came the first indications of progress on the German agreement and the SALT talks. About the same time, Secretary of Commerce Maurice Stans visited Moscow and brought back optimistic reports of potential billions to be made for American firms in the Soviet market.

For U.S. companies it was a signal that it was now patriotic to do business with Russia.

In 1972 the negative trade balance reached $7 billion. The large grain shipments to the Soviet Union that year and the expanding East-West trade in other areas changed this potentially dangerous trend. As Marshall Goldman puts it: "By the early 1970s a deteriorating economy at home had served to convert the attitudes of a surprisingly large part of the business and union communities toward increased trade with the U.S.S.R. Not only were sales to communist countries . . . generating more jobs for American workers and farmers and more profits for American business-men, but the one-sided nature of the trade flow enabled the United States to come close in 1973 to a positive balance in its overall trade dealings for the first time since 1970." By the time President Nixon began to assert that the era of confrontation was over and the era of negotiation had arrived, American multinationals were already looking seriously at the largest potential new market in the world—350 million customers in Eastern Europe and the Soviet Union and 800 million in China.

Soviet America-watchers believe that American multinationals played a crucial role in bringing about détente, because corporations needed better U.S.-Soviet relations to make it politically possible to do business in Russia and Eastern Europe. There is no doubt that Kendall, David Rocke-feller, and others who are doing business or wanted to do business with the Soviets constituted a powerful lobby for détente. When the Jackson Amendment, denying most-favored-nation treatment to the Soviet Union unless it permitted free emigration, was being debated in 1974, Kendall spent a good deal of time lobbying against it. According to congressional aides who heard his standard speech on the subject, he would attack the measure, which was designed primarily to benefit Soviet Jews, with heavy-handed warnings that such an interference with U.S.-Soviet economic rela-tions would lead to an outbreak of anti-Semitism in America. Nixon was shrewd enough to know that he could count on the support of multina-tionals for détente, but there is little evidence that the companies deserve any credit for the changes in strategic policy and geopolitical outlook that Nixon and Kissinger initiated. Commerce Department officials believe the Soviets are somewhat disappointed that the array of titans from the finan-cial and industrial world who make up the U.S.-U.S.S.R. Trade and Eco-nomic Council lack the power to keep détente on a steadier course.

In the 1960s the U.S. argument for increased trade with Russia was that better economic relations would improve political relations. Everyone agreed that, in strictly economic terms, the Russians had much more interest in the relationship than we did. What did they have to sell besides caviar? Just as the military relationship was until recently lopsided in favor of the United States, so also is the economic relationship between the two superpowers asymmetrical. U.S.-Soviet trade is more important to the Soviet Government than to the U.S. Government. This reality is reflected in the persistent and growing balance of payment and balance of trade deficit facing the Soviet Government. All calculations about the Soviet economy made in the West, especially projections, are dubious, because Soviet statistics are notoriously confusing to outsiders and are sometimes deliberately misstated. More important, the assumptions behind certain crucial figures may not be known. Nonetheless, the CIA has set up what amounts to an internal accounting firm to try to make such calculations. CIA specialists project a Soviet trade deficit by 1980 of $6 to $7 billion, which, if correct, means that the Soviets would have to take 25 percent of all the hard currency they earn on exports just to service the debt on their imports. (According to U.S. Government figures, at the start of 1977 the U.S.S.R. and the countries of East Europe owed the West about $39 billion.) Is the Soviet Union a good credit risk?

U.S. specialists on the Soviet economy point out that the Kremlin has been able to control trade imbalances that would imperil their credit by simply limiting imports by administrative fiat. Since the government has a monopoly on all foreign trade, this could be done, but, as the Soviet economy becomes more intertwined with the world economy, not without economic disruption and political cost. The Soviets are trying to ease their balance of payments problem by encouraging somewhat more tourism, expanding their merchant marine, and increasing their sales of gold. The Soviet Union is estimated to have about 2,000 tons of gold in reserve, worth at least $8 billion.

But the strongest card the Soviets hold is their petroleum reserves. Just as Soviet planners came to the conclusion that importation of American technology and American grain would continue for the indefinite future to play an important role in building the Soviet economy, the U.S. Government came to realize that growing dependence on foreign petroleum and raw materials was also an inescapable fact of life. The technology-for-petroleum swap now makes U.S.-Soviet trade a mutually advantageous proposition in economic as well as political terms.

The U.S.S.R., according to Alexander Sutulov's study *Mineral Resources and the Economy of the U.S.S.R.,* has about 12 percent of the world's oil reserves, 31 percent of the natural-gas reserves, and 47 percent of the world's coal. The United Nations estimates Soviet oil reserves at about 8 billion tons, double the estimated U.S. reserves. In czarist days Russia was a major oil exporter and continued supplying other countries after the revolution until just before World War II. The flow of oil virtually stopped in the postwar Stalin years. When his successors took over, they tried to throw off his autarchic policies and to expand the oil trade with the non-communist world, but they met fierce resistance from the Western oil companies, who controlled most of the world's pipelines, tankers, refineries, and sales and distribution networks. Little by little, however, the Russians, by undercutting the world market price, broke the oil companies' hold on such markets as Ceylon, India, Ghana, and Guinea. In 1957, after the closing of the Suez Canal, Enrico Mattei, the president of Italy's state-owned oil company ENI, began to import major quantities of Soviet crude oil and for many years thereafter was the Soviets' best customer for crude. Since the Russians first cracked the markets of the West, Finland, Yugoslavia, Sweden, Britain, and Japan have come to depend upon Soviet oil for a significant proportion of their total needs. By 1974 Soviet earnings on petroleum from hard-currency countries amounted to about $3 billion.

Although Soviet domestic production is increasing—the goal of the current Five Year Plan is to raise 1973 production levels by more than one-third in 1980—domestic use of oil is increasing at a faster rate. Stocks for export to hard-currency countries are declining. Thus the Soviet Union is also becoming a major importer of oil, originally from Algeria and Egypt, now from Iraq and Libya. They have extended more than $1 billion in loans and several billions more in military equipment to Iraq, Iran, Afghanistan, and Algeria. What these particular countries have in common is not ideology but oil and natural gas. During the aftermath of the 1973 Yom Kippur War, when the OPEC nations imposed a boycott on the United States, the Russians took advantage of the huge rise in the world market price and America's energy crisis to circumvent the boycott imposed by her Middle East allies. In 1973 the Soviets imported oil from recently nationalized Iraqi oil fields and offered it to U.S. importers. To avoid breaking the letter of the commitment to support the boycott, it appears that they shipped the oil to Romania for resale to the United States. They were also shipping the Arab oil to Czechoslovakia and Hungary to fulfill their obligations to those countries as a substitute for Soviet-produced oil originally intended for them, thereby making it possible to sell more of their own oil to the United States. It is difficult to trace the complex switching transactions that went on during the boycott, but Marshall Goldman concludes that it was more than coincidence "the the five-million-ton increase in imports from the Middle East to the Soviet Union in 1974 also happened to approximate the increase in Soviet oil exports to Western Europe, Japan, and the United States." Soviet economic interests—the need for dollars—prevailed over the temptation to capitalize on America's crisis. It is one example—West Germany's 1976 offer of a Christmas loan to stabilize the East German economy is another—that "interdependence" is more than a cliché. The web of economic relationships that tie nations together may create either advantages or disadvantages for one or another, depending on the circumstances, but it has made zero-sum-game diplomacy obsolete. It is naïve to think that economic relations can be arranged so that everybody always wins, but it is more foolish to believe that in a tangled world one rival's gain is always the other's loss.

One graphic illustration of the entangling economic relationships that now cross ideological lines is the pipeline system for the flow of oil and natural gas. Romanians are importing large quantities of oil from Iran through an Israeli pipeline that is the major conduit through which Iranian oil flows to Europe. It is not only to symbolize independence of the Soviet Union but to derive a crucial economic advantage that has made Romania the one country of Eastern Europe to maintain good relations with Israel. Knowledgeable European oil dealers claim that the Soviets have also received oil through Israel's pipeline. In the early 1960s the Soviets began to build a pipeline network of their own. The first pipeline was to Czechoslovakia, and the next, the Friendship Pipeline, linked Soviet oil fields to East Germany and the Baltic seaports. In the 1970s the Soviets have extended the Czech pipeline to make it possible to supply oil and natural gas to Western Europe. (Since the pipeline is entirely inside Czechoslovakia, East Germany does not have to be consulted about sales to West Germany.) A branch of the pipeline serves Northern Europe. The Friendship II Pipeline connects new fields in Siberia with West Europe. For many years Soviet oil sales to West Europe through the pipeline system and use of tankers have become increasingly important for the West Europe economy.

More recently the Soviets have opened overseas affiliates to refine and market petroleum products. With ELF-ERAP, a state-operated French oil company, they are building a refinery in Le Havre. Just before World War II the Soviets had about 10 percent of the petroleum market in

Britain, but these operations were eventually taken over by Texaco. In 1957 they began marketing petroleum products in Britain once more, and now Nafta GB, Ltd., a wholly owned subsidiary of the Soviet Ministry of Foreign Trade petroleum export division, runs 250 filling stations in London and southern England. The oil is refined in British Petroleum's refinery on the Isle of Grain in Kent.

The Soviets have a more ambitious operation in Belgium, a joint venture with two local coal-importing companies. Nafta B, as the company is called, has a large storage facility in Antwerp for storage of imported oil and is trying to buy a local refinery, but Belgian oil companies have so far resisted the attempt. The Soviet operation in Belgium acts in the manner of a capitalist multinational corporation by taking advantage of "worldwide sourcing." Thus Nafta B imports oil for the Belgian market not only from the Soviet Union but from the Middle East and other places. The Soviet Union is no longer just an oil exporter but an increasingly sophisticated middleman in the world petroleum market. Through the use of "swap sales" arrangements with Western companies the Soviets are able to expand their worldwide distribution network. Thus, to fulfill contracts to Japan, they traded 3.5 million tons of oil in a Black Sea port to a Swiss company in return for an equivalent amount in a Persian Gulf port. The Black Sea oil was hard to ship because of the closing of the Suez Canal, but there was easy access from the Persian Gulf to the Orient. These are just a few examples of how the Soviets are expanding their influence over the world petroleum market.

Natural gas is an even more important substance than oil for integrating the Soviet Union into the world economy. Soviet natural-gas fields are the largest in the world, containing over 31 percent of the world's estimated reserves. (The United States has about 15 percent.) The first Soviet natural-gas pipelines were built in the mid-1960s to carry the fuel to Czechoslovakia and Austria. In 1973 the pipeline network was extended to West Germany, and a year later to Italy. In December 1975 the Soviets concluded the largest gas deal in history, agreeing to supply 500 billion cubic feet a year of Soviet gas to West Germany, France, and Austria. By 1980 the supply to West Germany will equal their entire natural-gas consumption in 1970. By the same date the Soviets will be supplying the Italian economy with about 70 percent of what it consumed in 1972. With the opening of the pipeline to Finland in 1974, Sweden and Finland will also become increasingly dependent upon Soviet-supplied natural gas. It is estimated that by the mid-1980s Soviet exports of natural gas will equal

2 trillion cubic feet and will produce about $1.5 billion a year in hard currency.

Even larger natural-gas deals, involving the United States, have been the subject of prolonged negotiation since 1971. The North Star project is a proposed joint venture of a group of U.S. companies, led by the Tennessee Gas Transmission Company, part of Tenneco, and Brown & Root, the engineering and financing consultant firm. The project involves joint exploitation of the Urengoi gas field in western Siberia, reportedly the largest in the world. The gas would flow 1,600 miles through a pipeline to a plant near a northern Siberian port, where it would be chilled at a temperature of −260 degrees F. and turned into liquid. From there the liquefied gas would be shipped by twenty huge tankers to the United States, where it would be turned back into gas and distributed by the participating gas companies to customers in Pennsylvania, New Jersey, New York, and New England under a twenty-five-year contract. It is estimated that such shipments could supply 10 percent of the total needs of this market by 1982. The deal was discussed at both the 1972 and the 1973 summit meetings, and the Nixon-Brezhnev communiqué in 1973 mentioned it favorably. However, the deal in its original form did not go through because it required extensive financing by Export-Import Bank loans or government guarantees of commercial loans, and these were not possible after the Jackson-Vanik Amendment passed in April 1975.

There was considerable skepticism about the deal in Congress anyway. Senator Frank Church, chairman of the Subcommittee on Multinational Corporations, questioned whether so much financial risk of the project should be borne by the taxpayer. The Export-Import Bank would not be repaid until all the commercial banks had recovered their money. Then, too, there was always the possibility that the Soviets might cut off the supply of gas, which would not only cause a serious energy shortage in the northeast United States but would doom recovery of the investment. The companies argued that the North Star project "will generate a minimum of 250,000 man-years of employment in the U.S. in the period 1976 to 2007." As for the possibility that the Soviets would fail to deliver on their contract, Mr. Jack Ray, the top Tenneco executive involved, argued that the Russians "have been quite scrupulous in meeting the contractual obligations they have had on commercial trade."

This view of the Soviet trader as a hard negotiator but a scrupulous performer on contracts is generally corroborated by U.S. businessmen who have dealt with the Soviets and by Department of Commerce officials. But because of its size and strategic implications, this is not an ordinary commercial deal. "I find it a little hard to believe," Senator Church observed, "in a crisis that might develop between the United States and the Soviet Union that the Russian Government would not place its own interests above its contractual obligations and simply cut off the gas . . . It seems to me to be very naïve to assume that the Russians won't place their national interest first." But the Soviet economy itself would become so entangled in the gas deals that interrupting the gas for political reasons would be exceedingly difficult. For one thing, much of the gas is in remote areas of Siberia, so far from population centers in the U.S.S.R. that it cannot be transported except at astronomical cost to the domestic market. The gas is useful only for export. Second, the Soviet export program is tied to a substantial import program. By 1980 the Iranians will be supplying more than 20 billion cubic meters a year for the Soviet domestic market. The Soviets find it economic to import natural gas for certain parts of the Soviet Union. A unilateral cutoff would risk a retaliatory interruption of natural-gas imports.

The North Star project is a good illustration of the possibilities and risks of "linkage" strategies. Under normal circumstances the Soviets have increasing incentive to keep the world economy going so that they will continue to receive dollars for their gas, of which they have much more than they can use at home. But should they decide that overriding political interests warranted applying pressure on the United States, they would have two new weapons, default on a multibillion dollar loan and a gas embargo. No U.S. sheriff can seize a Soviet pipeline. The United States, with all its military might, did not have a very effective response to the OPEC oil boycott in 1973. Military threats would be even less effective against the U.S.S.R., which on rare occasions has interrupted deliveries for apparent political motives. The history of the North Star project shows that economic relations cannot be effectively manipulated by the United States for political purposes. When the possibility of public U.S. financing collapsed, Tenneco and the other companies obtained the necessary financing from West European banks backed by their governments. Some White House officials are concerned that the "leverage in reverse" on the U.S. Government by U.S.-based multinationals might become a serious problem if there is massive U.S. capital investment in the U.S.S.R. This would be especially true, they point out, in the event of a serious depression in the West, when economic relations with the Soviets and other nonmarket economies would become more important.

Armand Hammer has tried to put together an even more elaborate natural-gas deal, with participation of Japanese companies. A consortium of U.S. companies, Hammer's Occidental Petroleum, Bechtel Corporation, and El Paso Natural Gas, in cooperation with a group of Japanese business firms backed by the Japanese Government is seeking to develop the Yakutsk gas fields in central Siberia. The U.S. energy companies have signed an agreement with the Siberian Natural Gas Company of Japan to find the financing for this admittedly risky project—unlike the North Star project, the capacity of the oil fields at Yakutsk are unproven—and in March 1976 the Bank of America syndicated a loan of $25 million for the project, matched by a similar amount from Japanese state and private banks. This project calls for even more U.S. Government financing and guarantees than does North Star. After the exploratory phase, which originally required an Export-Import Bank loan of $49.5 million, comes the development stage, which was originally slated to involve the purchase of almost $4 billion worth of U.S. and Japanese equipment and technical expertise. About 45 percent of this amount was to have been financed by Eximbank loans. When completed, thirteen U.S. and Japanese tankers would deliver 1 billion cubic feet per day to Japan and a similar amount to the United States. This project involves considerable risk. The Export-Import Bank study shows that two-thirds of all the equipment will have to come from the United States. Since Japan does not produce the type of drill and rigs needed for Siberian conditions, there might not be enough gas to pay for it all. The Yakutsk gas deal is an example of the technology-energy swap at its clearest. The Soviet Union needs the technology from the United States and Japan to develop the resources for export to the two countries. There are uncertainties about what an advantageous price for the gas would be, given the extraordinary features of the arrangement and uncertainties about how long the supply will last. The Japanese are extremely eager to complete the deal since they depend upon imports for almost 100 percent of their oil and 73 percent of their natural-gas requirements, but the deal will not go through without U.S. participation.

Not only are U.S. technology and financing needed but there are political considerations that require U.S. involvement as well. The Chinese are strongly opposed to Japanese participation without the Americans. According to the Senate Subcommittee on Multinationals, "the Chinese Government has told Japanese leaders that the U.S.S.R. would gain too much political leverage over Japan if Japan does become excessively dependent upon Soviet natural gas projects. This danger in the PRC's

view would be somewhat diminished by official U.S. participation"—
presumably because the Soviets would not dare threaten stoppage of gas
sales that were financing repayment to U.S. banks and the U.S. Government. The specter of a Chinese-Japanese economic alliance that would
merge the technology of Japan with the resources and manpower of China
haunts the Soviet leadership and encourages efforts to offer Japan alternative economic ties.

Besides energy sources there are other raw-material contracts with the
Soviet Union which draw the web tighter. Perhaps the most spectacular of
these is another Armand Hammer deal. Occidental Petroleum has signed
a twenty-year contract under which the Soviets will supply 1.5 million
tons of ammonia, 1 million tons of urea, and 1 million tons of potash in
return for 1 million tons of superphosphoric acid. Such a barter arrangement in raw materials of strategic importance to their respective economies
gives each side leverage on the other.

From the Soviet standpoint the most important reason to subordinate
the isolationist impulse and to accept the vulnerabilities of entering into
interdependent relationships is to obtain technology from the West. A
recent study by a Birmingham University team, after reviewing the state
of Soviet civilian technology in electric power transmission, chemicals,
computers, iron and steel, machine tools, motor vehicles, oil drilling, and
process-control instruments, concluded that "in most of the technologies
we have studied there is no evidence of a substantial diminution of the
technological gap between the U.S.S.R. and the West in the past 15–20
years." Total Soviet production is still only half that of the United States,
and the average standard of living for Soviet citizens is about one-third
of the average American standard of living. Most economists now believe
that technological innovation is the single most important factor in promoting economic growth. By almost any measure the Soviet economy is
inefficient. Even the military sector, where the best brains and enormous
resources are committed, has not escaped the pervasive inefficiency of the
economic system. The MIG-25 which was flown by a defector to Japan
and then turned over to the CIA for scrutiny turned out to be much more
primitive in certain technologies than anyone had surmised. The CIA has
doubled its estimates of the real costs of Soviet military production, and
now estimates the defense budget to be about 11 or 12 percent of gross
national product rather than 6 or 8 percent as previously thought. The new
estimate is based not so much on substantial increased procurement as on
a new awareness of how little the Soviets get for a ruble.

There are many theories as to why the Soviet Union lags behind in technology. Some analysts concentrate on the continuity of Russian history as an explanation. Since the Industrial Revolution, Russia has always been behind, and she has always tried to catch up by buying technology in the West. It started two hundred years before Kosygin and Brezhnev, when Peter the Great traveled to West Europe to collect the advanced technology of the time. In the late 1920s the Soviets made substantial efforts to import technology. (In those days a German businessman with technology to sell was met at the Russian border in a chauffeur-driven limousine and taken to Moscow for negotiations.) In 1931 and 1932 over 2,000 German engineers and technicians went to the Soviet Union to help install and operate plants and machinery. But neither in Peter's time nor in Stalin's day could the import of technology be maintained or assimilated. Russia has been unable to maintain a continuous flow of technology from the West, and, after flirtations with technology transfers, has reverted to forms of self-sufficiency. This pattern has retarded economic growth.

The structure of Soviet society probably offers a better explanation for the technological lag than Russian history. The bureaucratic structure does not reward innovation on anything like the scale of capitalist societies. The pressure on scientists is administrative rather than competitive as in the Western societies. Orthodoxy becomes enshrined because practitioners of orthodoxy rise in the party. Risk-takers do not usually do well in the Soviet system. A former Soviet scientist living in Israel, Professor M. Perakh, thinks that the Soviet system contains antibodies that resist injection and diffusion of foreign technology. It is difficult to spread technical knowledge in the Soviet society, especially when it is obtained from abroad, because scientists are afraid to tell authorities the extent of the lag in their particular field. Thus Soviet researchers use foreign patents as a basis for research proposals "without disclosing this fact to fund-giving bodies or their own superior authorities." The scientist makes it appear "as if the idea were his own and was worked out in his laboratory," and the result is that a piece of research from the West is replicated without the authorities being aware of the fact. As Philip Hanson, a specialist on Soviet technology, points out, part of the Soviet scientific community has a "vested interest in halting or slowing both the introduction and diffusion of foreign technological information which would expose or render futile their own activities."

The conservatism of scientists is reinforced by the cautiousness of the plant managers, who, despite some recent efforts to increase their incentive for innovation, are primarily interested in meeting the short-term goals of the current plan, or possibly exceeding them and getting a bonus. New production techniques that disrupt current production can slow down production in the short term, and that is what primarily concerns the manager. The Soviet rule has produced some extraordinary economic achievements, especially economic security for almost everyone and virtually universal health services and education, but after sixty years the system has been unable to realize the potential of the enormous Eurasian land mass it controls or to come anywhere near making Russia a global economic power of a scale comparable to the United States. As Professor Herbert Block puts it, "Its economy has never matched its strategic capabilities; it is second in the world but a very secondary second."

American analysts disagree as to exactly when Soviet leaders decided to make a major effort to import technology. About a year after Khrushchev's fall in 1964, the State Committee on Science and Technology was organized and given the task of modernizing Soviet industry and technology. Kosygin's son-in-law, Gherman Gvishiani, now its head, was made vice-chairman. In the same year the first technological cooperation agreement with Fiat and the contract to build the huge Togliatti auto works were signed. Three years later, imports of machinery began to increase dramatically. By the end of the 1960s Brezhnev and Kosygin were hinting broadly in public statements that they considered the importation of technology important for building the Soviet economy. "The Communist Party of the Soviet Union," Brezhnev declared in 1968, "believes that one of our most important tasks now is to accelerate scientific and technical progress, to equip the working people with modern scientific and technical knowledge, and to introduce as quickly as possible the results of scientific discoveries."

Skeptics of détente attack the transfer of technology to the Soviet Union as the most politically vulnerable aspect of the relationship. Agreements to exchange technology between a highly developed and a much less developed society, they argue, are by nature something of a one-way street. True, the Soviet Union does sell technology in the West. In 1974 the Soviets were awarded 492 patents by the U.S. Patent Office, and in 1975 they had 25 license arrangements with U.S. firms for letting them use Soviet technology. As early as 1964 the Soviets licensed a surgical stapling device, which is safer and faster than traditional suture techniques, to the U.S. Surgical Corporation, and these instruments are now widely used in U.S. hospitals. There are a number of other areas in which Soviet technology is more advanced than that found in the United States or West

Europe. In metallurgy the Soviets have developed advanced processes for welding and casting of aluminum and a way of using low-grade alumina-bearing ore as a substitute for imported bauxite. They have made significant advances in iron and steel production and have sold technologically advanced blast furnaces to Japan, West Germany, England, and France. A delegation of the American Iron and Steel Institute visited Soviet steel mills in 1974 and reported that Soviet blast furnaces and coke ovens are superior to U.S. models. Soviet advances in hydroelectric power enabled them to outbid American firms on contracts to equip Canadian power stations in New Brunswick, British Columbia, and Manitoba. Together with Westinghouse they tried to bid on a contract to provide a new power station for the Grand Coulee Dam but were ruled out on national security grounds. The Soviets are ahead of everyone in developing hydrofoil craft which can be used as high-speed ferries. A U.S. firm is trying to start a shuttle service between the United States and Canada using Soviet hydrofoils, but the Jones Act, which outlaws the use of foreign-produced bottoms in U.S. commercial waterways, has blocked the project. Underground coal gasification and hydraulic mining equipment are other areas in which Soviet technology is of interest to U.S. firms.

But for the most part the United States is receiving in exchange something other than technology for the technical know-how it sends to the Soviets. Henry Kissinger argued that technology is one of the most important links for maintaining leverage on the Soviet Union since they want it badly and are becoming increasingly dependent on it. Such skeptics as Senator Henry Jackson say that the historic pattern will be repeated. Once the Soviets have acquired the technology they need, the isolationist impulse will reassert itself and the Russians will again withdraw from the world economy, but this time they will be stronger and more self-sufficient, in large part because of the technology the industrialized West has shared with them.

U.S. specialists, including Marshall Goldman, John Hardt of the Library of Congress, and Philip Hanson, see evidence that the present technological relationships with the West are much deeper and more pervasive than any developed in previous periods of détente. Goldman cites "the different nature of the new technology the Soviet Union is currently purchasing." It is far more complicated and fast-moving than in the past. It is more dependent upon spare parts. Especially in computers, chemicals, and electronics it is hard to duplicate. "The need to update technology," he points out, "is never-ending." There are many indications that the Soviets are planning for a continuing and expanding technological relationship with the West. In the 1930s a few dozen technicians worked at the Gorky automobile plant. About 2,500 technicians from the West went to build the Fiat plant at Togliatti in the 1960s. Pullman's Kama River project for building a huge truck factory employs 50 Americans at the site. An increasing share of the imported technology is for the export sector. Thus, when the Soviets import machinery for producing more cars than could be absorbed by the small domestic market, it appears that they are contemplating a long relationship. Since they must compete in the export market with the West, they are under continuing pressure to keep importing successive generations of new technology. John Hardt calls the new economic ties "continuous" and "long-term." The fact that the Soviets did not return to autarchy after the pretext given by the Jackson-Vanik Amendment suggests, Goldman says, the "the Soviet Union may already find itself interdependent." Soviet economists and trade officials have, he points out, expressed interest in joint ventures with U.S. firms "that would permit a continuing updating of technological developments in the West in exchange for some royalty sharing or other incentive arrangement." A leading Soviet economist told me that he and his colleagues are studying arrangements for installing American personnel as permanent quality-control officers in American-built factories. Each economic tie reinforces others and is part of a process that becomes harder and harder to reverse without great cost and internal dislocation.

Long-term technological ties are reinforced by the expanding network of Soviet banks. The Narodny Bank Ltd. of London has over $2 billion of assets and the Banque Commerciale pour L'Europe du Nord is one of France's ten largest banks. There are Soviet banks in Frankfurt, Beirut, Singapore, Kabul, Zurich, Vienna, and Luxembourg. The Paris bank created the Eurodollar market in the 1950s. Other banks engage in joint ventures with American and German banks. The Narodny Bank is part of an international consortium that includes Lehman Brothers, Bank of America, and twenty others in a $40 million project to build housing for the Iranian Navy.

But there are risks to sharing technology. Some have to do with national security. The skeptics argue that the United States is so far ahead in computer technology, for example, that almost anything the Soviets want would help them in their military programs. Their generals, U.S. intelligence analysts say, are particularly interested in miniaturizing electronic circuits to make their weapons lighter, more versatile and maneuverable.

Sophisticated computer technology could help them do this. Moreover, some, including Harry Schwartz of *The New York Times,* argue that any technological assistance for the civilian sector, even if it has no military significance in itself, makes it possible for the Kremlin to concentrate the best scientific talent on weapons technology.

It is difficult to see where the military technology race could make much difference to the outcome of any plausible U.S.-Soviet conflict, given the high state of technology and the enormous armaments levels on both sides. It could be more important in the case of wars between U.S. and Soviet clients who receive arms from the superpowers. Even marginal differences in tanks or airplanes could be decisive in such conflicts. But the strongest incentive to stay ahead or to catch up in the technology race is prestige. As the use of military power by nation-states becomes increasingly constrained, the symbolism of military power becomes more important. Being on the frontier of technology is more impressive a symbol than massive standing armies.

Thus the Pentagon continues to scrutinize technology contracts for possible military applications. In 1973 the Soviets were talking to Boeing, McDonnell-Douglas, and Lockheed about ordering ten 747s. Boeing, a leading defense contractor, did not have a single domestic sale that year and was eager for the business, but the deal was never made, largely for security reasons. Ironically, Senator Henry Jackson, Boeing's chief advocate in Congress, takes credit for helping to stop the sale. IBM contracted to sell a huge computer to Intourist for its reservation system, but the Pentagon stopped this sale too, on the ground that the Soviets didn't need such a big computer to take care of their tourists. Senator Henry Jackson argued that the KGB was so thoroughly intertwined with Intourist that the computer would end up as an instrument of social control. He successfully prevented the sale of a computer that made use of voice prints for crime-control purposes. Arthur Downey, who has been in charge of East-West trade at the Commerce Department, thinks that much of the heated discussion about selling the Soviets computers—the memory of sales of scrap iron to Japan on the eve of Pearl Harbor is sometimes invoked by the skeptics—is overdone. What is happening, he says, is that IBM is trying to sell Cadillacs when Chevrolets would do, and the Soviets like to do everything on a big scale anyway. There are easier ways for the Soviets to improve their military technology, he says, than to buy remotely related civilian technology. Besides, they can buy the technology in West Europe anyway. Richard Perle, Senator Jackson's aide, argues, on the other hand, that the Soviets are at least ten years behind in computer technology, and the United States has no particular interest in helping them to catch up. Such specialized technology as integrated circuits and wire memories can be used to build sturdier, more reliable weapons of greater range. While the CIA has the task of investigating the end-user for each questionable computer sale, there are over 2,000 cases waiting for such analysis. Citing Department of Commerce studies, Perle also argues that the United States is selling the Soviets technology at a bargain. In one case plans were sold to the Russians for $1 million which cost the U.S. Navy $2 million to develop.

Licensing technology to the Soviets, the national security question aside, is part of a larger problem. U.S. labor unions have for many years been concerned that U.S. companies are, for the sake of quick profits, turning other countries into archcompetitors by encouraging them to use American technology to take over traditional American markets. The result is a loss of jobs in the United States. The AFL-CIO has sponsored legislation that would empower the President to prohibit the export of capital and technology if it would adversely affect the U.S. job situation. Years ago Japanese electronics firms bought technology from the same firms they are now successfully challenging in many parts of the world. Skeptics question whether the United States should help the Soviet Union to compete successfully with U.S. firms. The Fiats built in Russia are already underselling Italian-built Fiats in some of the Italian firm's traditional markets. Some of the trucks being built at the Kama River plant, a project heavily dependent upon U.S. technology, are for export and will compete with trucks produced in American factories. General Motors now proposes to enter into an agreement with Poland to design and engineer a plant for a new line of vehicles, including light pickup vans to medium trucks, that will compete with the most sophisticated products of other automotive manufacturers in the West European market. Jack Baranson, president of Developing World Industry and Technology, Inc., points out that the strategy of multinationals is increasingly impelling them to share their latest technology with the countries of Eastern Europe, and eventually the Soviet Union too. "A growing number of U.S. firms have now decided," he says, "that the economic uncertainties and political risks associated with capital investments in overseas plants have become too high for realized rates of return." Therefore they are moving toward what he calls "a sustained enterprise-to-enterprise relationship" with foreign state-owned firms which will involve a continuing flow of expertise to enable the foreign enterprises to "design and engineer new generations of technology from the base acquired under the licensing agreement." This is a very different relationship from the 1930s model of building a plant in the Soviet Union and going home. Thus the product of certain multinationals is becoming technology itself, "the implanting of design and engineering capabilities which are the spawning grounds of future industrial competitors."

Paradoxically, the principal risk of extending crucial technology to the Soviets is that by so doing, the United States is helping to suppress the forces of reform inside Russia. Andrei Sakharov argues that supplying technology to the Soviets helps the rulers in the Kremlin to delay solving profound social and economic problems that they would otherwise be forced to confront. The Soviet Union, he says can amass political and military strength with outside assistance instead of developing the sources of inner strength—economic, political, and spiritual—which would be unavoidable if there were no help from the West. Only development through internal reform can change the repressive and stultifying climate of what he calls "this uncontrollable bureaucratic machine."

There is something to this argument. There is enough Soviet self-criticism to support the view of John W. Kiser III, a student of Soviet technology, that "the desire to circumvent some of their own systemic blockages is a major force behind the Soviet government's interest in acquiring Western technology." The rigid bureaucratic system inhibits technological innovation, which in turn retards economic growth, but the political costs of fundamental reform are seen as too high by the aging leadership of the Soviet Union. No one knows where a course of fundamental reform will lead. Therefore, when a Soviet technocrat such as G. Gvishiani tells a high U.S. Commerce Department official over drinks that "we will build a communist society in Russia with American know-how" he is saying more than he intends. Critics interpret his remark to mean "We will maintain the character of our rule with your help."

The advocates of increased technological exchange argue that the flow of information of all kinds has precisely the opposite effect. Arthur Downey points out that virtually every minister with responsibility for economic matters has visited the United States or has had extensive conversations with high American officials and businessmen in the last five years. It is now possible for businessmen to visit remote areas of the Soviet Union that were long closed to all foreigners. Several high officials have studied in the United States under cultural exchange agreements. A deputy minister of agriculture is a graduate of Iowa State University. These contacts are bound to have an effect on the thinking of the Soviet elite and to make it much more difficult to revert to the isolationism and paranoia of the 1950s.

Education through personal contacts has been a two-way process. Soviet officials seem exhilarated by conversations with such American technological entrepreneurs as Charles "Tex" Thornton and business planners such as Arthur D. Little and General James Gavin. American officials brought up on cold-war stereotypes have been moved by personal testimony of Soviet officials who privately acknowledge the shortcomings of Soviet society but radiate a patriotism and hope for the future which is hard to dismiss. One Soviet trade official described for his American counterpart how the system gave his father, an ignorant peasant, education, work, and dignity—which helped the American to see the Soviet Union with new eyes. Such conversations are easier to have in the context of economic and cultural exchange than in a world of high diplomacy or arms negotiations.

Nonetheless, it is now clear that the relationship between internal liberalization and economic growth is far more complex than observers in the West used to think, when it used to be said that "fat communists were contented communists" with whom one could get along. U.S. foreign policy, not only for Russia but for Brazil, Indonesia, Iran, and elsewhere, rests on the notion that a process of "embourgeoisement" within authoritarian regimes will eventually result in their liberalization. Bourgeois freedoms sooner or later emerge in a bourgeois economy. But, unfortunately, it is not inevitably so. Hitler raised the standard of living for the German people as he tightened the political control. The growth of the bourgeoisie in Brazil and Iran has hardly been accompanied by a growth of democracy. Indeed, Wolfgang Leonhard, a Yale professor, is probably correct when he says "the Soviet leaders have consciously initiated a policy leading toward rapprochement in order to *avoid* a liberalization of domestic policies"—not only economic reforms, the resistance to which we have already discussed, but political reforms enlarging the rights of Soviet citizens. There is much evidence for his view. At the Twenty-fourth Party Congress, held in March 1971, which set the new line on détente, Brezhnev outlined his own brand of linkage: his "peace program" would be linked to "an unabating ideological war." There have been many subsequent pronouncements warning of the need to maintain ideological purity and to combat the subversive ideas that accompany the goods and technologies from the

West. At about the same time that Brezhnev decided upon increased economic integration of the Soviet Union with the world economy as a strategy for growth, he tightened up on writers and artists and gave new powers and prestige to the secret police. (In 1973 Yuri Andropov, the head of the KGB was made a member of the Politburo.) Brezhnev reversed Khrushchev's "destalinization campaign" and, beginning in 1966, jailed some of the most gifted writers—Sinyavsky, Daniel, Ginsburg, Galanskov, Dobrovolsky—harassing Solzhenitsyn and his friend the cellist Mstislav Rostropovich and eventually driving them into exile. All intellectuals were warned to watch their step. "The Party and the People," he said at the Twenty-fourth Congress just as the breakthroughs on détente with the Nixon administration were about to be achieved, "have not tolerated and will not tolerate attempts—no matter what their origin—to blunt our ideological weapons, to stain our banner."

But whatever the intention to use domestic repression to reduce the political risks of interdependence, it has not worked out smoothly for the Soviet leadership. Détente, with its unjammed foreign radio broadcasts, thousands of tourists, businessmen, journalists, artists, and sports figures traveling in Russia, its intricate interconnected economic deals, and its new international obligations on human rights accepted at the 1975 Helsinki conference, has presented the Kremlin with a new reality.

Despite efforts to crack down on Soviet citizens in order to maintain social control in the face of increased foreign contacts, the strategy has not worked particularly well. *Samizdat* manuscripts, the privately circulated works of Soviet dissidents, have a wider readership than many published books in the United States. Every copy of a book in Russian from the West, according to Soviet sociologists who have emigrated to the West, has as many as 500 to 800 readers. Soviet citizens who used to turn on the soccer game now listen to the evening news on the Voice of America or the BBC. Andrei Sakharov and other prominent dissidents continue to be harrassed. Jewish demonstrators are jailed, usually for two weeks or less. Yet a number of dissidents are in regular contact with correspondents of *The New York Times,* and a few manage to give press conferences within the Soviet Union, denouncing Soviet authorities, without going to Siberia. Ordinary Soviet citizens invoke the pledges on human rights made by the Soviet Government to demand justice for themselves. There are now limits to what the Soviet Government can do to protect itself from uncontrolled ideological currents, and these limits are increasingly fixed by the reality that the world is watching and that foreign reaction, especially the increasingly negative reaction of foreign communist parties, cannot be ignored without serious political and economic cost. Yet there is a discouraging pattern in Russian history of opening the windows to the West for a time and breathing in new ideas from the West and then slamming them shut. Thus the imported liberalism of Catherine the Great at the end of the eighteenth century gave way to the repression of Nicholas I. Some of the ideas for which the "Decembrists," a band of constitutionalist officers, were shot had come to Russia with Catherine's blessing.

How much of a change in the American system will a prolonged, expanded, and increasingly interdependent relationship with the Soviet Union require? One former high State Department official in the Ford administration believes that if the United States is to expand its trade with Russia to any significant extent and open the way to significant amounts of Soviet imports, the American economic system is going to have to undergo some important changes. A market economy that is based on the private economic decisions of individual firms cannot interact with a centralized state-controlled economy except to its disadvantage. It must tighten up the system. If trade with nonmarket economies is to play an important part in the American economy, the U.S. Government will have to play a bigger role.

One major problem arises from the peculiar pricing structure of the Soviet economy. There is virtually no link between internal prices and prices in the outside world. As Raymond Vernon, professor of international business management, explains it, "The price of wheat inside the Soviet Union may be very cheap in relation to the price of automobiles, at least by the standards of the rest of the world; yet that fact creates very little strain for the U.S.S.R. Its agents are still free to buy wheat and sell automobiles in foreign markets on a pattern that would seem perverse or impossible for most countries in the West." U.S. tariffs, taxes, and subsidies for foreign trade are based on the assumption, as Vernon points out, "that domestic costs and prices play a causal role in international transactions." There have already been problems determining what is a price in the United States for goods that do not have a domestic price determined by market forces. Domestic manufacturers are worried about "dumping"; they are afraid that the Soviet Government will set artificially low prices on manufactured goods exported to the United States to undercut domestic competition. There has already been a small crisis involving Polish-made golf carts.

Another problem is the opportunity that the competitive system gives the Soviets to play one firm off against another. The Soviets don't accept this as a problem because they see the U.S. economy as a form of "monopoly capitalism" in which there is little price competition anyway. Professor Vernon calls this "primitive" Soviet view an obstacle to the development of a framework for mutually advantageous economic relations, for the Soviets seem to think that foreign trade in the United States, conducted by privately owned monopolies, is not essentially different from the conduct of Soviet trade, which is dominated by state-controlled monopolies. Given the fact that much of Soviet trade has been with the oligopoly industries—oil, metals, makers of power plants that do not compete with one another on price—their perception is not wholly wrong. Nonetheless, as we shall now see, there are important areas in which the interests of individual firms differ and in which they do in fact compete, and it is here that the opportunity arises for state trading monopolies to play one firm off against another. This raises the question, as Vernon puts it, "of how far the United States is prepared to centralize and control its trade with the Soviet Union in order to insure that the interaction between the two economies brings adequate benefits to the U.S. side."

The Great Grain Robbery of 1972, as it is now inevitably known, is the most famous example of the careening of a state monopoly into the private market. Except for the confrontation with the Soviets in the 1973 Middle East war and the dispatch of Cuban troops to Angola in early 1976, no incident had so shaken public support in the United States for the Nixon-Kissinger détente as the 1972 grain deal. The irony is that the Russians behaved shrewdly but correctly, well within the established rules of the game at the time. The disaster occurred because of the stupidity, and in some cases the venality, of American officials.

In July and August 1972 the Soviet Union bought over 19 million tons of grain in the United States worth $1.2 billion, 433 million bushels of wheat, 246 million bushels of corn, and 37 million bushels of soybeans. The wheat was purchased at a penny or two below the market price at the time, which was about $1.61. But within weeks the unprecedented purchase caused the market price to double. A year later wheat was selling for more than $5.00 a bushel. Within a few weeks the Soviet grain-purchase delegation, headed by Nikolai Belousev, chief of Exportkhleb, the Soviet company for exporting and importing grain, cornered one-quarter of the U.S. wheat crop. Much of their success was due to the secrecy with which they operated. The Department of Commerce did not disclose the presence of the Soviet team to the public, and each grain dealer, as is customary, tried to keep his sales secret from the others. The Soviets obtained a $750 million credit from the Commodity Credit Corporation of the Department of Agriculture to finance large purchases after a cash purchase of 8.5 million tons had already been concluded.

The purchase has been called a robbery because it did not reflect the real bargaining power of the parties. The Russians had suffered a crop failure of monumental proportions. The U.S. agricultural attaché in Moscow reported to Washington in the spring that a bitter cold, almost snowless winter and a late thaw had led to the loss of one-third of the Soviet grain acreage. *The New York Times* of April 13, 1972, reporting on a visit by Secretary of Agriculture Butz to Soviet farms in southern Russia, quoted U.S. officials as saying that the estimate of a 30 percent crop loss was "conservative." Thus not only were the Soviets in a weak position to buy grain at a bargain but U.S. officials were aware of this fact. Yet they did not inform the U.S. purchasers or make use of the information in their dealings with the Russians. The Russians were so intent upon disguising their true position that on July 10 they turned down 600,000 tons of wheat from the Bunge Corporation at what was in fact a bargain because the price was supposedly too high. The secretary of agriculture and other leading officials later testified that they had no precise idea of what was happening with respect to either the Soviet harvest or the negotiations with the American grain exporters.

The 1972 wheat deal caused bread and beef prices to shoot up around the world and added significantly to the inflation crisis of the early 1970s. Extensive investigations by the House Committee on Agriculture and the General Accounting Office not only revealed a failure to make use of available intelligence about the Soviet bargaining position or to show elementary business shrewdness but also induced a strong suspicion that agriculture officials were making use of inside information. It is a tradition in the American system for regulators to shuttle back and forth from the industries that they regulate. F.C.C. commissioners turn into broadcasters, Federal Power Commissioners run electric utilities, and so on. But it is rare that these career transformations are so precipitous or so vulgar. Clarence Palmby, assistant secretary of agriculture, accompanied Secretary Butz to Moscow in April to inspect Soviet crops and to negotiate with Soviet officials about credit and imports. A month earlier he and his wife had purchased a condominium in New York City, having in mind a job with Continental Grain, a job Palmby had been repeatedly offered in January, February, and March. Shortly after returning from Russia, Palmby resigned from the Department of Agriculture and the next day went to work for Continental Grain. Palmby testified that he showed the Russian grain negotiators around the city of Washington on July 2 and sat in on three days of negotiations. Continental sold 60 percent of what the Soviets bought on their summer 1972 shopping trip.

Clifford C. Pulvermacher, another high official in the Department of Agriculture, also accompanied Butz to Russia. He was offered a job by Bunge, another large grain exporter, while the Soviets were still in the country negotiating the large purchase. Bunge did not succeed in selling anything to the Russians until a week after Pulvermacher decided to accept the job. Carroll Brunthaven, who replaced Palmby, had been an executive of Cook Industries, another of the big grain exporters to the Soviet Union. Despite being informed by Continental Grain officials of their sales to the Russians, he failed to inform either farmers or the general public about what was happening.

Inside information was important for several reasons. First, those officials who knew that the Russians were out to buy large quantities of grain were in a position to benefit particular companies by passing the information along. Continental Grain sold over 8.5 million tons of grain for cash, according to the House Committee on Agriculture testimony, before some of the smaller companies even knew the Russians were in New York. Inside information as to the size of the purchases enabled the same companies that were selling large quantities of wheat to buy grain or grain futures before the price shot up. Good connections in the Department of Agriculture also helped grain dealers take maximum advantage of the subsidy program. Until the program was ended in the uproar over the Soviet grain deal, the Department of Agriculture pegged the domestic price of grain higher than the world market price, and, to encourage exports, paid subsidies to the sellers equivalent to the difference. The world price was set at $1.63 a bushel, and the subsidy was calculated on the difference between this figure and the market price at the time the grain was actually shipped and the sale registered with the Department of Agriculture. By signing contracts for sale in July and waiting to apply for subsidies until late August, Continental made as much as $.47 a bushel in subsidies. Estimates made before the Senate Committee on Government Operations indicate that about $316 million in subsidies went to the large grain dealers in the summer of 1972, about $160 million of it attributable to the Russian purchases. When the Department of Agriculture ended the subsidy program on August 24, 1972, it gave the companies advance warning and an extra five days to obtain the extra $.47 a bushel, although there was no apparent justification for it. During those five days 167 million bushels were registered for the subsidy at a cost to the taxpayer of $78.5 million. It did not help relations when Deputy Minister of Foreign Trade Vladimir S. Alkhimov offered in 1972 to resell the Americans some of their wheat at triple the price, observing that "after all, we bought the wheat at market prices. They have been low, but look at Alaska, which we sold you for $7 million back in 1867. That was cheap too, but you don't hear us complaining."

Both countries seem to have learned something from the grain deal. The Soviets now provide more information about their harvest. (The United States, it should be noted, gives the Soviets information about their own agricultural conditions by making available photographs from reconnaissance satellites.) The United States requires better reporting from the grain companies. U.S. officials are now convinced that the government must coordinate huge sales on the scale of the 1972 grain deal. Private companies cannot adequately represent the interests of consumers and taxpayers. In October 1975 an agreement was reached with the Soviets under which they would agree to purchase a minimum of 6 million tons a year for five years, and no more than 8 million without consulting with the U.S. Government. From August to October 1975, while the agreement was being negotiated, the United States imposed an embargo on all grain sales to the Soviets, which infuriated the farmers, who thought that the government was actually negotiating the price of their wheat behind their backs. Some of the officials involved in trying to regularize the agricultural sales with the Soviets speculate that their efforts may have cost President Ford the election, since farmers in 1976 were still smarting over the embargo and the reasons behind it, which Kissinger insisted upon keeping secret. (The nomination of Robert Dole for Vice-President was to placate the farmers, but he alienated a good many others in crucial states.)

Even the 1972 grain deal was not all one-sided. It helped shipping and farm-equipment companies and caused a favorable shift in the U.S. balance of trade. But it demonstrated that without government intervention individual companies are susceptible to pressure to make deals that sacrifice larger public interests for easy profits. Doing business with the Soviets has certain aspects of a lottery. There is a low probability of making a deal for most firms that try, but a high payoff if they succeed. I remember talking to some exhausted members of the Italian team that negotiated the Fiat contract in 1966. They were on the brink of success, but all they could talk about was the two years they had spent in hotel rooms and waiting rooms hoping for a sign that a breakthrough would come. Even now there are several large U.S. companies waiting for a big deal: International Paper was invited to bid on a $1.7 billion pulp and paper complex in Siberia, which Soviet officials say is still under consideration if credit can be found. Kaiser Aluminum and Alcoa lost a bid for a $220 million alumina refinery to the French, but Alcoa still hopes to build a $500 million aluminum smelter. About eighteen U.S. multinationals have offices in Moscow which cost from $100,000 to $500,000 to set up, and as much as several millions more to staff and support. Companies complain that making proposals for the Soviets is especially expensive because they require all sorts of details not usually demanded by U.S. or European purchasers. Then, too, there are quixotic aspects to the negotiations. An American businessman may suddenly be asked to come to Moscow on the next plane and then be told to wait in his hotel room, a tactic, businessmen suspect, to induce them to sign anything just so they may return home. But despite the annoyances connected with doing business in Moscow, most representatives of U.S. firms now living in the Soviet capital have great respect for the Soviet representatives with whom they deal. As a rule they are well informed and know the international market. They haggle over the contract terms but have a good record of observing the strict letter of the contract once it is signed. When Soviets are buyers the record seems at least as good as normal commercial standards. When they are sellers, according to a 1971 report of The Conference Board, deliveries are sometimes unreliable and products occasionally do not "live up to the samples on which the purchases were made." *Aviation Week and Space Technology* reported that Aeroflot, the Soviet airline, has pirated passengers from Pan Am by issuing tickets contrary to their agreement. But examples of Soviet failure to perform on commercial contracts are rare indeed.

Doing business with the Soviets is an experience that differs widely from industry to industry. The biggest disappointments have come to those companies such as International Paper that have invested considerable time and money in the hopes of landing a huge contract, but have had such hopes dashed because the Soviets want credit and U.S. law now makes that impossible. Vladimir Alkhimov, the deputy trade minister, likes to tell U.S. visitors that the U.S.S.R. is getting over 10 billion credits from West Europe and Japan and consequently they are getting the big orders.

U.S. companies that deal with the Soviets in products not requiring massive foreign financing are doing well. Dow Chemical, which has been buying naphtha from the Soviets since 1962, does over a $100 million a year trading chemicals. The Dow representative calls on sixty foreign-trade organizations selling everything from herbicides and pesticides to chemicals for plastics and acquiring a range of raw materials in return. Virtually all of this trade is in barter form. Representatives of Soviet ministries with whom one negotiates, most businessmen in Moscow agree, are well informed about the market but have little room for bargaining.

All such factors—the original cost of establishing a Moscow office, the prospects of enormous deals, the frustration of waiting—create temptations to give away too much in commerical dealings. Marshall Goldman notes that American businessmen "seem prepared to offer terms and make concessions to the Russians they would never dream of making to our older and more traditional trading partners." In an effort to get a foot in the door, U.S.-based multinational banks, including Chase Manhattan, have offered loans in Eastern Europe at rates below those they charge commercial borrowers in the United States. Some of the euphoria of the early 1970s, when U.S. businessmen (encouraged by the Nixon administration) saw East-West trade as a source of tens of billions, is gone, but they still see in the huge land mass that stretches from Stettin to Vladivostok an enormous potential market, one that could become especially important in the event of another depression in the West.

There are powerful economic and political pressures operating in both the United States and the Soviet Union to expand economic relations. If this happens, it will force important changes in business-government relations. Some, like the grain agreement, have occurred already. Most specialists in East-West trade argue that the government must actively coordinate the activities of private firms, even the giants, when they deal with the Russians to avoid one being played off against the other. Antitrust laws that forbid collaboration and price-fixing, they say, should be waived so that companies can get together and present a common front to the Russians. Marshall Goldman has suggested that the United States needs a wheat board such as the Australians and the Canadians have, to handle the sale of wheat to the Soviet Union and Eastern Europe. High officials in the State Department note that independent agencies such as the Maritime Commission can now pursue policies at odds with State Department positions and warn that East-West trade can turn into a nightmare unless there are ways to enforce a government-wide position on important policy questions.

The logic of tighter controls on East-West trade is irresistible, but the effect will be to reinforce and accelerate negative trends that are already transforming the U.S. economy. One is concentration. A few small companies, it is true, have done well. Lerch-Hubbell, Inc., a tiny door manufacturer in Cheektowaga, New York, has a $500,000 contract to supply door fittings for the Soviet trade center, which is a $110 million project to build a complex that includes a 20-story office building for foreign trade representatives, a 2,000-seat conference hall, and two hotels with 1,225 rooms. Holcroft Company, of Livonia, Michigan, owned by another small company, Thermo Electron, made a contract to supply furnaces for the Kama truck plant which represented in 1972 half of all the business done by the parent corporation. But for the most part only large corporations can incur the expense and find the credit needed to do business with the Soviets. Thus, if East-West trade becomes more significant in the U.S. economy, it will further promote bigness. If government intervention into the private commercial dealings of U.S. multinationals becomes more important, particularly if antitrust provisions are waived, the role of competition in stabilizing the U.S. economy will become even weaker than it is now.

One of the supreme ironies of the U.S.-Soviet rivalry is that each in its effort to preserve its own system has borrowed heavily from the other. To fight the cold war the United States completely restructured the federal government, concentrating power in the executive, promoting secrecy and clandestine operations, cutting away Congress' constitutional role in making foreign policy, instituting loyalty procedures, and authorizing the widespread violation of civil liberties once held to be the essence of American citizenship. Each of these changes mirrored a Soviet institution and each was designed to put the United States in a better position to oppose Soviet power. Even the classic Russian institution of a large peacetime standing army has been copied in the era of the cold war. For their part, the Soviets have tried to imitate American management techniques and American technology to increase their power *vis-à-vis* the United States. It now appears that expanded East-West trade will require the United States, which has already borrowed ideas from the Soviet state, to borrow some ideas from the Soviet economy as well.

CHAPTER 7
The Rigors of Coexistence

Détente is a vague word for a specific stage of development in the sixty-year relationship of the two entangled giants. There have been, as we have seen, a series of little détentes that briefly bloomed and withered during three generations of coexistence. But in the Nixon-Brezhnev years something new happened. The elites who manage the two continental empires recognized their mutual dependence. The stability of their own rule required a *modus vivendi,* a reality not clearly perceived before. In the years when the United States enjoyed unchallenged global military and economic preeminence, transforming the Soviet Union, even ending communist rule, did not seem beyond reach. The rapid growth and transformation of postwar America was built on the idea of a permanent anticommunist crusade. At the height of the cold war even the word "coexistence" was suspect. Soviet leaders always believed that they needed coexistence but were unprepared to pay a price for it because they distrusted the West and feared to reveal their own weakness. Like the Americans, they used the tension of the cold war for internal development.

By the late 1960s the struggle of the two elites to understand each other had taken a new turn because external events had radically altered their relationship. Each nation had achieved the capability of incinerating the other. America's forward thrust through military action had been stopped. Soviet ideological hegemony over the "socialist camp" had been challenged. Both societies were suffering a crisis of legitimacy: in the United States the disillusionment of the Vietnam War, Watergate, domestic spying, racial tension, unemployment and the end of the boom; in the U.S.S.R.

mounting cynicism about the shallowness of the ideology, the inefficiency of the economy, the corruption and crudeness of the bureaucracy, and the pervasiveness of repression. Both systems seemed to be afflicted with what some American critics of U.S. foreign policy call a "failure of nerve"— a weakening commitment to the principles on which the societies were founded and a confusion about direction.

Neither nation has the power to remove its rival or to control its internal process of transformation, and the elites on both sides recognize this. Both understand the need to avoid a nuclear war but they also realize that this goal cannot be achieved without developing alternative entanglements. Avoidance of war alone is not a strong enough foundation for prolonged coexistence.

Kissinger's web of coexistence was woven of economic, technological, and cultural strands but it is fragile because the United States–Soviet relationship is not symmetrical. The Soviets consciously borrow from the United States—technology, managerial know-how, style. But Americans, even those who would like to see fundamental changes in the system, have little interest in the Soviet model. Americans, however radical, unlike those of the 1930s, do not think the Soviet Union is the future or even that it works very well. Nevertheless, there is a growing convergence of interests between the two societies that is strengthening the web.

Both are preoccupied with security problems that transcend the rivalry between them. For the United States elite the growing threat is the weakening of American control over the world economy, the uncertain access to raw materials, and the spiraling costs of running the most complex industrial civilization on earth. The Soviet Union is in a position to exacerbate America's problems if it chooses, and occasionally to profit from them, but it has very little to do with the process of decline of American power against which the managers of the American Government are seeking to develop new strategies.

The managers of the Soviet Union are beset by a number of threats— the hostility of China, mounting ideological challenge from dissidents, from communist modernizers within and without. The consequences of a frozen revolution—bureaucratic rigidity, a weakening economic pulse, rising cynicism—add to the unresolved problem of the old Russian empire —how to maintain control over a huge land mass of many nations, languages, and cultures without an idea that legitimizes the centralization of power. The United States is not the source of any of these problems. Indeed peace with the United States is probably crucial to the solution or even the effective management of all of them. The Soviet elite needs more than technology and credits from America. It needs the breathing space that only the United States can give.

The competition between the United States and the Soviet Union has certain aspects of a war, but, fortunately, there are no clear war aims on either side. Neither America nor Russia has a plan for national salvation such as Hitler's obsession to erase the humiliation of Versailles by taking all of Europe or Japan's ambitions for a Greater East-Asia Coprosperity Sphere. For much of the last generation the United States had clearer and larger ambitions than did the Soviet Union, a *Pax Americana* backed by a preponderance of military might and economic power.

Despite its formidable economy, its network of military installations stretching around the globe, and its self-proclaimed mission to guide internal political development in the Third World, with military interventions if necessary, the United States lacked the inner confidence either to press for victory over the Soviets or to develop ground rules for long-term coexistence. The Soviets competed impressively in rhetoric but almost nowhere else. In the cold-war years the five oceans were American lakes to the extent the nation wished to incur the expense to make them such. American forces were stationed on every continent. Until the 1970s U.S. military or paramilitary forces were involved in a foreign military operation or a coup roughly once every eighteen months. But the Soviet Union has yet to send combat troops outside the empire it claimed for itself in World War II. Thus, neither in arms, money, nor influence were they a match for the United States. For much of this period the United States ran the arms race with itself.

The cold war was confusing because the United States and the Soviet Union were playing different games. Only one was a world power that saw its security tied to the development of a global economic and political system in which it would have the dominant voice. The other defined security much more modestly, but pursued the limited goals aggressively— tight control of neighboring territory, development of deterrence capabilities, building the economic and military base for an expanded world political role in the future.

In the late 1970s we are in a new situation. The rivals are not only more nearly equal in military power (though still far apart in geopolitical and economic terms) but they are also drawing closer in their definition of their respective roles in the world. It has been fashionable to talk about convergence of the American and Soviet systems as a historical process that could bring greater accommodation between them. The danger is that convergence will have precisely the opposite effect. The Soviets have begun to imitate American techniques for projecting power—foreign bases, aircraft carriers, and proxy wars. Each military system spawns a social system dedicated to justifying its use. Military bureaucracies are developing in the Soviet Union that are mirror images of American bureaucracies. Their expansion risks the further militarization of policy.

The Soviet Union is becoming more of a world power, but the process is slow and cautious. Up to now their ambitions have been modest, ending the twin policies of containment and self-containment and opening new options for relating to the world and playing a bigger role in guiding its affairs. They have not been aggressive in inserting themselves into the "global issues"—relations between the industrialized and nonindustrialized worlds, revamping of the world monetary system, development of a world energy policy, etc. At the United Nations and other international bodies that discuss such matters they are surprisingly passive. American diplomats who follow their activities believe that the Soviets see no advantage in identifying with either the Third World countries or the rich ones, though on crucial votes they tend to line up with the latter.

The managers in the Kremlin have been cynical about revolutions in other countries. Their sixty-year history is a record of how easily their revolutionary zeal on behalf of others has been sacrificed to the interests of the Soviet state. But Soviet activities in Africa suggest that Soviet support for wars of national liberation may increase. In part this is happening because there is enough of the old Bolshevik in the Kremlin bureaucrats to excite them about being instruments of a world historical process of revolution. Support for liberation movements abroad is also a legitimating principle for a regime that has lost touch with its own revolutionary roots. Just as it is easier to promote human rights abroad than at home, it is easier to agitate for revolution in other peoples' countries. But mostly, it is old-fashioned geopolitics.

At this point Soviet use of military force outside its borders still does not compare in scale to American efforts. But the more the Soviets imitate the Americans' role as a great power, the greater the danger of a violent clash of the giants. The Soviet military buildup alarms American planners and an American public that has been educated to believe that their own security rests on the mystical notion of being "second to none." As the Soviets increase their military power and appear to abandon some of their caution of earlier years, White House Soviet experts worry aloud about a

Russian John F. Kennedy pledged to get the country moving again. The old men who rule Russia are veterans of the Second World War, and its horrors are stamped on their consciousness. The next generation, unsobered by war, brought up on a Soviet version of the politics of *grandeur,* may be tempted, they speculate, to leap over intractable domestic problems by taking the classic route of foreign adventurism.

The war that no one wants will come by miscalculation. It will spring from a conviction that it cannot be avoided. Such a war psychosis pervaded both societies in the late 1940s and early 1950s, at a time when only the United States had a real option to launch a first strike. The greatest impact of the idea of détente has been to break the mind set of inevitability of war. The danger of a failed détente is that it reinforces the pessimistic premise that no peace is possible.

The threat of unintended war is growing. One reason is that the huge complex war-preventing system we call deterrence, in which millions participate, hundreds of billions are spent, and political energies absorbed, is increasingly subject to outside interference—proliferation of nuclear weapons, terrorism, new and subtle forms of monkey wrench politics. Nuclear weapons are not merely in new hands; they have become intertwined in an entirely new set of problems. The game theory model persists, but there are now too many players at the table; one can no longer count on the old rules being observed.

The second reason for alarm is that the military competition between the United States and Russia is becoming increasingly unstable. The SALT negotiations have not succeeded in slowing the arms race. While the diplomats talked, stockpiles of nuclear weapons on both sides doubled, and major advances in military technology, such as the cruise missile MIRV (multiple warheads) and MARV (maneuvering re-entry vehicles of increased accuracy) were introduced. The compromise SALT II agreement which the Carter administration hopes to achieve, a resolution of a long deadlock on how to handle the cruise missile and the new Soviet Backfire bomber, marks the end of a long era of negotiation. In itself it does not open the way to serious disarmament, or curb the "mad momentum" of the arms race. While arms controllers have been preaching "stable deterrence," the military environment has become much more threatening to both sides. The emphasis on increased accuracy of missiles suggests an intention to target enemy missiles, and that implies a willingness to strike first or a belief in the possibility of fighting controlled nuclear wars. The introduction of the cruise missile, which can be concealed in an ordinary bomber, opens the way to deliver a virtually limitless number of nuclear warheads on the Soviet Union from forward bases surrounding its territory. Military planners on both sides have plausible arguments to build more weapons and to plan quick reaction, pre-emptive strategies to prevent their own missiles from being destroyed in a surprise attack. For any rational political leader, war is indeed unthinkable, but huge military bureaucracies in the two countries are paid to think about it every day, to plan for it, and to develop scenarios for "winning." The madness of one bureaucracy sustains the other. The technological nightmare into which we have entered is an environment that chokes rational thought.

But it is not only technology that threatens to upset the elaborate chessboard on which the cold war has been played. The complacency about the arms race is rooted in the feeling that since there has been only one atomic war since 1945, it is not going to happen again. The next thirty years, however, will bear no resemblance to the generation that has just ended. Political instability is increasing on a global scale. The era of *Pax Americana* which collapsed in the Indochina War was a time, for all its crises, of extraordinary stability. Because of its growing prosperity and its hold on the levers of world power, the United States could play a global managerial role. Europe and Japan, war-weakened, were amenable to various forms of American influence. The Soviet Union was a very junior giant. Today every western economy faces a long-term economic crisis with high unemployment and inflation, the classic sources of social instability, which economists neither understand nor know how to manage. The global competition for scarce resources and for markets is intensifying. The desperation of the poor Third World countries, which a generation ago were only objects of world politics, is increasing, and with it their capacity to destabilize a complex and interdependent world economy.

The Carter administration correctly sees that these so-called "north-south" problems—managing the tensions within the non-communist, industrialized world, finding ways to restore their economic and social stability, developing a common front *vis-à-vis* the non-industrialized nations (those with natural resources to sell and those without)—pose far greater challenges to the survival of the American way of life than the Kremlin's master plan, whatever it may be.

In his campaign Jimmy Carter criticized Kissinger for being too absorbed with the U.S.–Soviet relationship and too pessimistic about the kind of bargains a strong and confident America could strike with the adversary. Within the first six months the new President declared, "Being confident of our own future, we are now free of that inordinate fear of Communism which once led us to embrace any dictator who joined us in our fear." Upon taking office, the new Director of the Central Intelligence Agency gave a balanced appraisal of Soviet strengths and weaknesses. It reinforced the new optimism of the Carter administration that the United States, for all its problems, is so much stronger than the Soviet Union that it need no longer make détente the centerpiece of its foreign policy.

The Soviets have the same perception of their relative weakness. Except in the military area, where the Soviet Union is catching up, the United States is in a different league. Through its worldwide relationships, it controls capital, technology, and natural resources beyond anything the Soviets can approach. Its domestic economy is much stronger, its geopolitical reach more impressive, and its society more stable.

The United States now runs the risk of exaggerating and minimizing the Soviet challenge at the same time. The dynamics of the arms race leads inevitably to alarmist projections of Soviet military capabilities and intentions. At the same time the evident interest of Soviet leaders in avoiding confrontations and their past willingness to back down—as in Cuba, the Middle East war, and elsewhere—when confrontations do occur inspires a complacency within American leadership that may be unwarranted. If the possibilities of creating positive entanglements with the United States recede, and the arms race takes the giant step forward that appears to be in prospect, then the likelihood of confrontations will increase. There are too many opportunities for scoring points in a politically unstable world for the Soviets to forswear the classic game of imperial politics they are playing, for example, in Ethiopia. If they perceive the "correlation of forces" shifting again to a newly confident, activist United States, they may well believe that spreading Soviet influence wherever opportunities open up is an essential "defensive" strategy to counter the "strong and confident America" the new President celebrates in his speeches. Herein lie the greatest dangers of miscalculation and unintended war.

There will be no possibility of a lasting détente without a fundamental change in the military relationship: not a modification of the arms race but an alternative security strategy based on a realization that the risks of the present security arrangements are far greater than the risks associated with comprehensive disarmament and demilitarization of the anachronistic rivalry between the United States and Russia. Elites on both sides may pretend that they can find security without building new forms of dependence upon the other, but they are wrong. Each is a prisoner of a sixty-year obsession which cripples the possibilities of liberating either society. The most urgent security threats facing the giants come not from each other but from the systemic crisis each faces at home.

Further Reading

Arbatov, G. "Concerning Soviet American Relations." *Pravda,* April 2, 1976 (reprint from U.S.S.R. Embassy).
——. "Maneuvers of the Opponents of Détente." *Pravda,* September 4, 1975 (reprint from U.S.S.R. Embassy).
Barron, John. *KGB: The Secret Work of Soviet Secret Agents.* New York: Readers Digest Press, 1974.
Blechman, Barry M., and Fried, Edward R. "Controlling the Defense Budget." *Foreign Affairs,* January 1976.
Senate Committee on Foreign Relations. "U.S.S.R. and Grain." Washington, D.C.: U.S. Government Printing Office, 1976.
Conquest, Robert. "A New Russia? A New World." *Foreign Affairs,* April 1975.
Draper, Theodore. "Détente." *Commentary,* October 1974.
Finley, David D. "Détente and Soviet-American Trade." *Studies in Comparative Communism,* vol. VIII, nos. 1, 2, Spring/Summer 1975.
Gaddis, John Lewis. *The United States and the Origins of the Cold War, 1941–1947.* New York: Columbia University Press, 1972.
Gavin, Gen. James M. "Soviet Trade—and Multinationals." *Duns Review,* September 1972.
Goldman, Marshall I. *Détente and Dollars: Doing Business with the Soviets.* New York: Basic Books, 1975.
Grossman, Gregory. "An Economy at Middle Age." *Problems of Communism,* March/April 1976.
Harriman, W. Averell, and Abel, Elie. *Special Envoy to Churchill and Stalin 1941–46.* New York: Random House, 1975.
Holzman, Franklyn D. *International Trade Under Communism.* New York: Basic Books, 1976.
Ivanov, I. D. *Multinational Corporations in the World Economy.* Moscow: 1976.

Joint Economic Committee. "Soviet Economy in a New Perspective." July 17, 18, 19, 1973.

Kalb, Bernard, and Marvin Kalb. *Kissinger*. Boston: Little, Brown & Company, 1974.

Kennan, George F. "After the Cold War: American Foreign Policy in the 1970's." *Foreign Affairs*, October 1972.

————. *Memoirs 1950–63*, vol. 2. Boston: Little, Brown & Company, 1967–72.

————. "United States and the Soviet Union 1917–1976." *Foreign Affairs*, July 1976.

Kissinger, Henry. "Central Issues of American Foreign Policy." *Agenda for a Nation*. Kermit Gordon, ed. Washington, D.C.: The Brookings Institution, 1968.

————. *Nuclear Weapons and Foreign Policy*. New York: Harpers, 1957.

————. *The Troubled Partnership: A Re-appraisal of the Atlantic Alliance*. New York: McGraw-Hill, 1965.

Leites, Nathan. "The New Economic Togetherness: American and Soviet Relations." *Studies in Comparative Communism*, vol. VII, no. 3, Autumn 1974.

Morris, Roger. "Détente Is in the Eye of the Beholder." *New York Times Magazine*, May 30, 1976.

Newhouse, John. *Cold Dawn*. New York: Holt, Rinehart and Winston, 1973.

Nixon, Richard M. "Asia after Vietnam." *Foreign Affairs*, October 1967.

Pipes, Richard. *Soviet Strategy in Europe*. New York: Crane, Russak & Co., 1976.

Rosencrance, Richard. "Détente or Entente." *Foreign Affairs*, April 1975.

Schlesinger, James R. "A Testing Time for America." *Fortune*, February 1976.

Schurmann, Franz. *Logic of World Power: An Inquiry into the Origins, Currents, and Contradictions of World Politics*. New York: Pantheon Books, 1974.

Shulman, Marshall D. "Relations with the Soviet Union." *Agenda for a Nation*. Kermit Gordon, ed. Washington, D.C.: The Brookings Institution, 1968.

Tatu, Michel. *Power in the Kremlin: From Khrushchev's Decline to Collective Leadership*. Translated by Helen Katel. London: Collins, 1969.

Ulam, Adam B. *Expansion and Coexistence: The History of Soviet Foreign Policy 1917–67*. New York: Praeger, 1968.

Index

ABOUT THE AUTHOR

RICHARD J. BARNET is a founder and codirector of the Institute for Policy Studies in Washington, D.C. He has been a Fellow of the Harvard Russian Research Center and of the Princeton Center for International Studies and has taught at Yale and the University of Mexico. During the Kennedy administration he served as an official of the State Department and the Arms Control and Disarmament Agency, and was a consultant to the Department of Defense. He is the author of several books, including *Global Reach: The Power of the Multinational Corporations* (with Ronald E. Müller), *Who Wants Disarmament?*, *Intervention and Revolution, The Economy of Death,* and *Roots of War.*